W.O.W. 2000

How To Turn Employees Into Owners
How To Create a Profitable Concept
How To Find the W.O.W. Niche
How To Change

Barry M. Cohen

edited by James D. Scurlock
Savannah Corp.

FIRST EDITION

ISBN Data

Cohen, Barry M.
  W.O.W. 2000: How To Turn Employees Into Owners, How To Create A Profitable Concept, How To Find The W.O.W. Niche, How To Change/ Barry M. Cohen - 1st ed.

  ISBN 0-9657602-0-0
  Business/Economics/Finance

To my wife Donna,

I love you.

ACKNOWLEDGMENTS

I am privileged to have had many great teachers who entered my path through life. They taught me whatever they could, and hopefully we grew from each other along the way.

The first person is Donna my wife, from whom I've learned how to become a softer, gentler person and develop my personal High Touch abilities. She has done an amazing job of "mellowing me out" from my days of growing up in Brooklyn, N.Y.. She is my partner and my best friend in my personal matters as well as my business world.

My children Logan and Lindsay have taught me to accept every person as their own individual. Their ability to love me even though I was gone working in my career while they were growing up has made it easier for me to stay focused on why I needed to become successful.

Then there are my parents, Leonard and Rhea Cohen, from whom I learned the gift of giving and being involved in the Community. They gave me my drive to create WOW in everything I did, especially those that were extra-curricular in nature. I am very pleased to be able to share this book with you. You taught me how to be responsible for my own life and I took your advice—probably too much. You have my promise I will do a better job. I love you both.

To my brother Shelly and his wife, Ginny and our niece Dana. I've made many mistakes throughout my career and in no way did I intend for any of it to ruin our relationship. I am totally focused on repairing this and getting our families to know each other and build a family bond. I am committed to do whatever it takes.

My in-laws Don and Kate Hall--and to all my Florida Family--Thanks for everything you've done to help my family while I was working all the time. I love you all.

James Scurlock is a genius. He constantly teaches me about business and marketing. As you will read, he made this vision a reality. He worked endlessly into the wee hours of the morning writing the final edits. Thanks James. You're the best. I know that Brandon Robertson worked closely on the manuscript as well—thanks for your help.

P.A. Geddie is a miracle maker. She was actually able to pull my thoughts and interpret my logic so that we could start the writing process. Thank you for all of your time and endless effort, to make this project a reality.

Then there's the Kern family--Dr. Jim, Denise, Katie, Jamie, Pam, Paul and Chris; Carrie and her husband Martin Phillips. They taught me the value of relaxation, family values, and the cost of procrastination. Jim taught me the importance of sharing my knowledge and findings with others, he has been a nationally known speaker for many years and has allowed me to share my vision, argue my opinions and help mold my thoughts. Knowing you is an honor, sharing with you is always a pleasure and I truly value every minute of your time.

Pat, Eileen, Michele, and Jesse Maginnis--It's over twenty years of friendship, Pat. It's been an incredible journey. Your urging and ideas have helped me stay focused and your creative genius has helped direct this project. Thanks for all of the time and effort.

To my stockholders: Billy J. "Red" & Charlene McCombs, Henry A. & Jan Reed, Carrie Postolos, Gary & Glenda Woods, Suzanne & Todd Davis, Michael C. Majors, Sadie R. Majors, Dan & Chrissy Anthony, Carol

Ann & Lynn Hunt, June L. Boldt, Ima Chavez, Robert Frank, Rufus E. Parker, Eugene R. Reinhart, Richard Sanchez, and Joe Villarreal, Jr.. Thank you for the opportunity to learn, grow, develop, create, fail, succeed, and change. Our partnership approach has allowed me to develop a clear vision to take us down the road for the next 28 years.

To my corporate office: Pam, Gail, Diana, Jan, Diane and Chris. Your dedication, ownership, commitment to excellence, ability to do whatever it takes and be there whenever it counts are what has made us the best. Thanks for all of your support and hard work.

I am blessed with fantastic general managers: Mike Couling, Gary West, Judith Graves and Jeff Holden, as well as great managers, TEAM Leaders, and employees with whom I work, and from whom I've learned great lessons on leading for the 21st century. Their urging has helped me mold the philosophy and allow me the focus on those few things I do best, as they empower others to do what they do best. Together we are developing a model future—and helping each other continuously learn.

Mentors have been an important part of my development, and having constant exposure to so many talented people over the years has helped guide me to where I am today. Thank you Zig Ziglar, Norman Brinker, Richard Melman, Mort Meyerson, Tony Jeary, Aaron Fodiman, Barry Brown, Doug Ditton, Tom & Jan Tracy, T. Scott Gross, Herb Kelleher, Tullos Wells, Joe Krier, Bill Mock, Jim Reed, Richard Maiewski, Leon Cikota, Allen Dreeban, Scott Hawkins, Julie Staten, Robert Pope, Jim Chism, Donnie Freedman, Ron Boatwright, George Postolos, and Dr. Dennis Stiffler, to name a few.

Having an opportunity to co-author my first book with a team of people I truly admire and hope to be half as good as was an honor for me this year also. Your commitment and dedication as leaders in the foodservice industry is greatly admired. Thanks for including me in "50 Proven Ways to Build Restaurant Sales and Profits": Bill Marvin, Gloria Boileau, Susan Clarke, Howard Cutson, Tom Feltenstein, Peter Good, Jim Laube, Bill Main, Phyllis Ann Marshall, Rudy Miick, and Ron Yudd. Your years and mastery of the hospitality industry has made an impact on my strategies and beliefs in life. I look forward to sharing many future opportunities together.

To Les and Diana Shenker, my pals from Southampton College, Peter Dittman, Larry Lennox and Marshall Siegel. I have not forgotten what you have done for me during my journey through life. Repayment for these lessons are in the near future.

Juanell Teague is really an angel in disguise. You taught me how to guide, direct and find my passion, and made sure I specialized and learned all I could about my topic. Your ability to create the journey for people to focus on their vision is amazing. I will never forget my "Servant in Leadership."

Relationships with vendors have been an important part of my success, and will be even more important to my future. Thank you AmeriClean Systems: Stephen Stingle, Tracy Galloway, Jimmy Carter, Keith Ashley and Jim Forrester for your dedication to my W.O.W. 2000. Also Alliant Foods, Paul Conley, for catching the vision and committing Nestle as a sponsor, as well as providing Old San Francisco with a great win-win relationship, the ultimate goal.

To Ellen Koteff of *Nation's Restaurant News* and Glenn Withiam of Cornell University: thank you for publishing my articles and helping spread the W.O.W. vision.

Thanks also to the employees of Southwest Airlines, who have kept me on schedule, and, often, kept my spirits high along the way.

Finally, to Phil Ratner, Charlie Amato, Gary and Glenda Woods, Mac and Kathy Stringfellow, Robert and Cathy Anderson, Susan and Bob Neiman, Sonny and Linda Melendrez, John Raslowsky, Joe and Tina Haynes, Lewis and Mary Kroll, Al and Belinda Silva, Tom and Judy Rosel, Milton and Flora Porterfield, Bob and Judy Bomer, Dr. Charles Miller, Andy and Cheryl Barkley, and everyone from Sales and Marketing Executives, the Chambers of Commerce, the American Heart Association, the San Antonio and Texas Restaurant Associations, Freedman Foodservice, Edward Don and Company and everyone else who there wasn't space to mention. Without you none of this would have been possible. The value of one's life can only be measured by what it has meant to others. Thank you for giving me so much.

WHAT DO YOU NEED TO KNOW TODAY?

INTRODUCTION

The times, they are a changin'.

Bob Dylan

Change is no longer incremental. Change is revolutionary. Where fundamentals used to shift over a period of years or decades, they can now undergo quantum leaps in a period of months, and often do. Consider the millions of coffee bar aficionados created by Starbucks Coffee overnight, or the hundreds of millions of consumers around the world who are now "wired" to the Internet. Starbucks has propelled a quantum leap in lifestyles, while the World Wide Web has revolutionized the way we communicate with one another. Each has done so in less than a few years.

W.O.W. 2000 will teach you the new fundamentals of our fast-paced, "fast-food" modern culture. It will show you how to meet the challenges of the year 2000 and beyond, transforming revolutionary change into profitable opportunity. Unfortunately, most of us feel so overwhelmed by the *speed* of change that we do little or nothing at all to revolutionize our businesses; we are still hiding within the security of outdated practices and "niche" marketing paradigms. But to survive in the next several years, we can no longer hide. We must reach out of our organizations to touch our customers, our employees, and our communities. W.O.W. 2000 shows you how.

As I was writing this book, it became obvious that we cannot change our organizations if we are not willing to also change ourselves: our thinking, our actions, and our relationships. In the 1990s, people can expect to make seven major career changes before they retire, so most of us have come to realize that change is inevitable. Still, too many of us fail to go the next step and actually *embrace* change before we are forced. But none of us—even "Old" San Francisco—can afford to wait for our customers to tell us that we're outdated. We must create our own changes.

Why should you listen to me? I have dedicated the past twenty-five years of my life to the hospitality industry. My first job was working in a deli in a Brooklyn neighborhood, where I learned some timeless lessons about customers, business and people in general. Since that time, I have stayed within the restaurant industry as a chef, general manager, owner, investor, chief operating officer, and, finally, chief executive officer of Old San Francisco Corporation, the parent of one of the highest-volume concepts in the industry. I have worked for companies which thrived due to superb management, as well as those which failed due to dishonesty and terrible planning. In the past twenty years, I have literally served millions of people, from those who couldn't afford a tip to the world's most famous superstars. For me, it has been a long road, filled with every conceivable emotion and lesson.

This book is the culmination of all of those experiences. Although I have been keeping extensive records of my different careers—both to teach others as well as to remind myself how to remain successful—I realized that there are only three principles that really matter: "W.O.W.", "High-Touch", and "Consistent Effort." These three principles form the backbone of my philosophy; they are directly responsible for the success of every organization I've ever managed. You will find definitions of each in the following pages; as you read into the book, I doubt that there is a chapter which does not mention at least two. They are that pervasive and that important.

Had I simply listed these three principles, however, this book would make for very dull—and probably much less effective—reading. I have therefore illustrated each principle and lesson with at least one story; if you are currently involved in the hospitality industry, you can already relate to most of them. In any case, I hope that you can realize the book's lessons without actually experiencing the sometimes painful consequences which make them so enduring and powerful in my own mind. It is, after all, the wise man who can learn from the mistakes of others.

Finally, I hope that this book provides you with the inspiration to change the way you do business. That is not to say that you may not already be doing an admirable job; in fact, most of us are doing the best that we can today. But what really matters is whether or not we find opportunity in tomorrow's changes. I am confident that W.O.W. 2000 will show you how.

Barry M. Cohen
San Antonio
March 1997

This book is divided along five major challenges: management, financial, marketing, vision and leadership. After each challenge, you will find a collection of chapters on a single topic which is relevant to your business today: trends, pioneers (companies which have made significant changes), street smarts, and technology, to be precise. The management, financial and marketing challenges sections are each followed by a summary of the W.O.W. 2000 lessons, as well as a "check-up": a line-by-line comparison of where your business is today versus where it needs to be in the future.

You may decide to go directly to the chapters which interest you most; however, I would suggest reading this book straight through at least once. This will allow you to complete a "course" in W.O.W. 2000. The various sections where I have solicited your input will make much more sense this way, and you can literally tailor the book to improve your own organization. No two businesses are alike; by entering data which is specific to your business, you are creating your own "W.O.W. 2000" plan.

There is another way in which to use this book, and that is by sharing its lessons with others. I have kept each chapter relatively short so that many people in the same organization can read several sections a day without imposing much of a burden on anyone's schedule. During the period of writing W.O.W. 2000, discussing the ideas with my managers, employees and investors proved invaluable. A book can be a very useful tool in bringing people together, and I hope that W.O.W. 2000 can serve that purpose within your organization as well.

PART I

W.O.W. 2000 PRINCIPLES

W.O.W.

HIGH TOUCH

C.E.

WHAT IS W.O.W.?

The more you do to create an impact,
the less you need to do to obtain success.

Patrick Esquerre, founder, La Madeleine

Wow is a familiar term. For decades, customers have used the word "wow" to describe an experience which not only exceeded their expectations, but took those expectations to a completely new level. We talk of being "wow"ed by a terrific dining experience, or, alternatively, of "wow"ing our guests with the unexpected. Wow is an emotional reaction which leaves an indelible mark in our memories. As Patrick Esquerre hints above, "wow"ing customers means creating an impact that, in turn, begets success.

Whenever I discover a successful company, I inevitably find people who are experts at creating such impacts. Las Vegas, where we license a restaurant, is a terrific example. The "WOW" casino/hotels, such as "New York, New York" (which boasts replicas of the Gotham City's most famous landmarks) and The Mirage (fronted by a volcano which explodes in extraordinary light and fire every thirty minutes) are always packed with thousands of tourists. Next door, however, you'll find the rubble of an older hotel which lost its luster years ago. While the newer hotels are creating a lot of excitement and impact, many—but not all—of the older ones are dying away. The same phenomenon can be observed in virtually any industry today. The choice is clear: "wow" your customers, or fall by the wayside.

Before we set out to create the "latest and greatest" concept, however, we must have a working definition of "wow" that makes creating high-impact part of our daily business routine; we must therefore transform "Wow" the experience into "W.O.W." the *discipline*. I define "W.O.W." the discipline as the following:

W.O.W. is the discipline of creating a measurable and lasting impact.

W.O.W. has become an invaluable part of every business today because exciting and entertaining our customers are both integral parts of any successful concept. Plenty of companies can provide good products and warm service; few can create the kind of impact which turns a concept into a thriving enterprise, or, better, a legend.

Old San Francisco Steakhouse is such a concept. Originally founded nearly thirty years ago at the World's Fair in San Antonio, our five restaurants "wow" customers with their 1890s Barbary Coast antiques and memorabilia, their dueling pianos on massive bars, their huge blocks of Swiss Cheese on every table (we are the largest non-grocery buyer of Swiss cheese in the country), their endless loaves of hot sourdough bread, their cavernous dining areas (our largest dining room has over 500 seats) and, of course, the daring performance overhead by the "girl on the red velvet swing": every forty-five minutes, one of our "swingers" boards a velvet swing attached to a thirty foot ceiling; as the pianos roll to a crescendo, the swinger reaches full stride, and she kicks two cowbells attached to opposite sides of the ceiling. Talk about eatertainment!

I was fortunate to join the Company after its legendary reputation was well-established, but I soon realized that we could not rest on what had been 21 years of success, no matter how great. So, while we maintained the special touches that our steakhouses are known for—the girl on the red velvet swing, for example—we also set out to find what would create a "wow" impact on customers today and tomorrow. This book contains a lot of what we found, and it tells you how to create "wow" practices in your business. It is up to you to apply these practices, and, hopefully, develop new ones. The essence of W.O.W., after all, lies in doing what has not been done before.

But isn't "W.O.W." a phenomenon impossible to define in business terms? Yes, and no. "W.O.W." capitalizes on the intangible desires which we all share to be surprised, excited and even pampered. But I am convinced that "W.O.W." can be made into a discipline, because that is exactly how we have achieved (and sustained) our success at Old San Francisco.

In order to better understand exactly how "W.O.W." works as a discipline, it is helpful to remember three principles:

- Be **W**atchful of New Opportunities and Changes
- Be **O**pen to New Ideas Beyond the Traditional
- Be **W**illing to Take Risks and Do It Differently

These principles should serve as a guide as you implement W.O.W. in your business. They should help you understand how to create the impact for your guests, employees, vendors, and the communities in which you live and work. As you will see, W.O.W. is not just about successful marketing, but applies to innovating your management and financial practices. To paraphrase Sergio Zyman, marketing chief of Coca-Cola, Inc., W.O.W. is "no longer a part of what we do. It is what we do."

WHAT IS "HIGH-TOUCH"?

"High Touch" is the second principle of *W.O.W. 2000*. Simply put:

High Touch is the art of producing a personal impact which goes beyond the confines of the traditional business relationship.

"High Touch" is a universal practice which should apply in all of your relationships, whether with customers, employees, members of the community, vendors, or even competitors. Being "high touch" requires both a willingness to understand those who shape our success, and the courage to take action when we sense an opportunity to touch someone in a way that will be especially meaningful to them. A few recent examples:

- *The founder of a large chain of restaurants visits his original location. During a brief walk through the kitchen, he recognizes a long-time employee who he has not seen for 10 years. The founder, touched by the employee's dedication, gives him the $300 in his wallet to say 'thank you.'*
- *A regional chain of steakhouses partners with a large airline to save a group of stranded teenage volunteers who are far from home, then throws them an appreciation party. The airline and steakhouses foot the entire bill.*

- *A man and his wife show up an hour late for their table at a restaurant. Because their table has now been given to another party, the host calls a competitor's restaurant, makes the reservations, and pays for the couple's meal at the other restaurant.*

These are all real examples--two of them are from our company, one is from a friend's. In each, the initial benefit might be hard to discern, but the care was genuine and the result a lifetime employee or customer.

Unfortunately, many larger companies discourage "high-touch" by instituting strict policy guidelines, and eliminating the ability of their people to be spontaneous. While many of these companies may very well believe that their policies—such as making their servers kneel down while taking a table's orders, or writing their name on a paper tablecloth—are high-touch, these policies are most often gimmicks with little to offer in the way of substance. Customers understand when employees are making an extraordinary effort in order to provide wonderful service, just as our communities know when we make a serious commitment in a time of need. "High-touch" is incredibly effective precisely because people recognize sincerity.

I always know when we have achieved "high touch" in our restaurants because people tell us immediately. They use phrases like "I can't believe that you all did that." or "No one has ever treated me as well as you did." People can, in fact, get very emotional when they call or write to thank us for making their visit especially memorable. I have listened to customers cry because we cared to provide very small extra touches that made their special moments unforgettable. In fact, Old San Francisco is consistently ranked one of the most romantic establishments in the country because our servers have coordinated so many marriage proposals, earning their customers standing ovations from literally hundreds of other guests in the dining room (a favorite place to propose is on the "bar swing" at the front of the restaurant). We must be one of the only casual dining establishments in the country routinely entrusted with engagement rings.

Although I offer a definition of "high touch" above, the only way to truly understand it is by practicing the principle within your existing relationships. The chapters ahead offer many examples of "high touch"; use them as a guide to revolutionize your relationships with everyone around you.

C.E., which stands for Consistent Effort, is the *W.O.W. 2000* work ethic. At Old San Francisco, we train our employees that "W.O.W." and "High-Touch" are both unattainable unless we put forth the effort, day in and day out. Since our business is creating a customer experience, C.E. means doing whatever it takes to ensure that every one of our guests leaves our restaurants with a positive impression. So the quality of the effort we produce matters just as much as the quantity.

C.E. is certainly not a new concept, but it is easily forgotten. When we lose sight of the importance of consistent effort, we allow ourselves and our employees to fall into the trap of the quick-fix: instead of concentrating on working hard throughout every day, we search for golden bullets that will create dramatic surges in business overnight. Take the restaurant industry, as one example. Plenty of concepts experience initial success, but few are able to achieve profitability year after year. What happens? Management fails to put forth the effort needed to keep its customers happy *every day.*

More than any other principle, consistent effort has been the key to sustaining Old San Francisco's success over the past 28 years. We have learned that the following equation

E=MC^2 [Effort = More Cash (or Customers)^2]

is an accurate predictor of our future success, not a gimmick or motivational technique. Whenever we increase the amount of effort on the left, we receive more of whatever we want to achieve (customers, cash or virtually any other payoff) on the right. Of course, we may not be able to predict exactly when the payoff will occur, but, after almost three decades of solid sales and profits, we know that it will.

Finally, C.E. doesn't mean that we don't believe in working smarter. We do—in fact, W.O.W. 2000 will teach you how to re-focus your efforts on "high pay-off activities", which will turn your C.E. into increased sales and profits. Too many of us still work eighty-hour weeks to simply keep our heads above water.

A friend in the industry recently put it this way: "Success in this business is hitting a bunch of singles and doubles. Occasionally, we'll hit a triple, or maybe even a home run. But if we can keep batting singles, we'll continue to grow and be profitable."

Part II

The New Management Challenge:
Turn Employees Into Owners

Understanding the Management Metamorphosis

Once upon a time, managers were the superheros of corporate America. Decked out in the uniform of the pressed white shirt and dark suit, they commanded immediate and automatic respect.

Times have changed. Employees now run our businesses. More often than not, managers are simply warm bodies along for the ride, with a key to the front door and a lot more headaches than the rest of the crew. Instead of being respected, they're resented. It's no surprise, then, that management positions are basically there for the taking at most establishments. Employees increasingly see "management" as a bad deal: a much greater amount of responsibility for a relatively modest increase in compensation.

The results of this shift have been disastrous: inferior managers with miserable lifestyles, demoralized and disrespectful employees, and few solutions to a minefield of new issues which we've never faced before: sexual harassment, multi-lingual workplaces, single mothers who take their small children to work, and repetitive stress syndrome, to name a few.

From this seemingly overwhelming litany of problems, however, a management metamorphosis is emerging at successful companies. Within these progressive organizations, senior managers are becoming more involved and more "high touch"; lower-wage employees are being given unprecedented incentives, and even stock ownership; diversity is finally being leveraged as a positive, not a recipe for hopeless confusion; and managers are beginning to listen more than command. The definition of management itself is changing.

One of my favorite examples of the modern management metamorphosis is Paula Lambert, the founder of the Dallas Mozzarella Company. In a few short years, Paula has managed to transform a tiny production facility and a dozen or so workers into an internationally acclaimed producer of cheese. Today, she sells millions of dollars worth of goat cheese, mozzarella and specialty cheeses to demanding clients around the world.

But the real accomplishment is an extraordinary working relationship which Paula, a former debutante, has built with her employees, who are overwhelmingly Spanish-speaking inner-city residents. How did she overcome the obvious cultural and language barriers to build one of the most quality-focused teams anywhere? First off, she realized that her English was outnumbered. So she learned working Spanish. Then she went a step further, because she knew that "high touch" with her people required learning their traditions, not imposing her own. When Christmas came around last year, Paula Lambert hired a mariachi band to entertain her employees around a traditional Mexican feast. I happened to visit the store on the day of the party, and it was pretty clear that she knew her share of the songs and dances. I doubt that anyone has done as effective a job with their people, or had as good a time doing it, as Paula.

Understand Your Employees' Priorities

The old paradigm says that employees have only two concerns: advancement and money, in that order. The old paradigm is wrong.

Today, employees possess a limitless number of concerns. Ask a dozen of your people why they work for you, and you'll probably get a dozen different responses, ranging from "I need to pay for my car insurance, because my parents don't", to "I'm paying alimony for three kids, and this is my second job." I have employees who have tailored their work schedule to acquire very particular things, such as gold-rim wheels for their car, college tuition for their kids or family vacations.

We cannot manipulate our employees' priorities to fit our needs, but we can help our employees define their needs in terms of our priorities. In doing so, we eliminate communication breakdowns, we create much more effective incentives, and we avoid being irrelevant to our own people, because we understand their priorities as well as our own.

Granted, it may seem incredibly strange to you that a thirty-year old man would rather live at home and drive a fancy car than begin a life on his own and ride the bus. It may seem utterly ridiculous that a twenty-five year-old would spend $500 on a set of gold-plated wheels for his pick-up truck. But people are living with more social pressures to acquire specific things now than ever, whether the right "car" or the right pair of sneakers for their kids. The bottom line is that those are their priorities, not yours. Help them achieve what's important to them, and they will help you achieve what's important to you.

Management is the art of influencing those who make the organization work: our employees. Success is therefore a function of their performance, and not ours.

There are basically three types of employees we can choose from: mercenaries, loyalists or partners. Partners are by far the best.

Mercenaries are those employees who you pay to do a job. They work a certain number of hours at a certain level of effort, and you write them a check. This includes temporary and outsourced workers, but also the kind of employee who is just working for the paycheck at the end of the week. In any case, the mercenary could basically care less what happens to the company, as long as his check clears.

Loyalists are the opposite of mercenaries. They work because they have an emotional attachment to their job, and to you. Of course, if you didn't pay them anything, they'd eventually move on. But what really matters to them is the feeling of attachment. Perhaps they've joined a start-up firm, which is very exciting. Or they've worked at the same company for decades, and it's become their identity. For whatever reason, their identity is heavily invested in their job.

Partners lie somewhere in between the two. Money is important, but so is the job itself. The partner chooses the Company carefully, because he feels that it offers a special opportunity--perhaps the business is growing, or he's simply heard good things about it from his friends. Where mercenaries do no more than they are told, and loyalists do far more (sometimes, far more than you'd like them to do), partners tend to do what they feel is in the company's best interests. They will take responsibility for their tasks, but they will also explore ways in which to make the Company better.

I have witnessed companies which outsourced everything to mercenaries, and I have seen those that value loyalty above all else. Both frighten me. While the mercenary companies limit their ability to provide excellence by outsourcing their standards of customer performance, the loyalist companies often seem out of control. Why? They're usually headed by egomaniacs who have little idea what they're doing, who surround themselves with loyalists so that their own authority will never be challenged.

Good employees, like good partners, will be drawn to your company for both rational and emotional reasons. They will demand a fair pay structure, but your ability to be "high touch"—your commitment to principles, and the values you reflect by your treatment of others—will ultimately matter more to them. Best of all, they will see your success, your commitment to doing whatever it takes, and your customer focus, as examples to follow. Partners want to be part of an exceptional team from the start.

It is no surprise, then, that we find our best employee-partners by referral from existing employees. They know that Old San Francisco is a fair, honest and fun place to work. They also know that they want to keep it that way—they'd rather work with friends and partners than mercenaries.

Ever heard of a ZORK? Probably not.

A ZORK costs $250,000, looks an awful lot like a sugar caddy, and it's your job to sell it to a group of executives from the largest companies in the world. Sound like a tough sell? Maybe. But if you apply for a job at Old San Francisco, you'd better be prepared to convince my managers that the ZORK is an invaluable asset, worth every penny.

Why? Because if you succeed at selling the ZORK today, tomorrow you'll be selling a table of our customers a $20 bottle of wine, or a $4.95 Bananas Foster. And if you've proven that you can generate enough enthusiasm and excitement to sell something fictional for $250,000, we're pretty confident that you'll make the sale on a wonderful bottle or a tempting dessert. That sale makes a huge difference. Let's say, for example, we do 400 covers one night, and our waitstaff "sells" an additional 100 bottles of wine, or 400 desserts. That's another $2,000 in sales per night, or over $700,000 per year. Talk about sales building!

Phil Romano, founder of a number of successful concepts, encourages his employees to sell by giving customers the chance to taste and see the menu before buying—one reason that his latest venture, Eatzi's, is "WOW"ing customers to the tune of $250,000 a week in sales. Like most restaurants, of course, we can't allow customers to sample every dish before they decide, so our servers have to "WOW" them with descriptions instead. The items on our menu are actually very much like the fictional ZORK, insofar as customers must rely on our descriptions. So our ability to build our sales depends on our servers' abilities to create the tastes, the smells and the appearance of the food with their words.

And they do a terrific job. Our check average of $28 is more than double the industry norm of $11 or so. But does that mean our employees are more than twice as friendly or intelligent as the industry norm? As much as I'd like to think so, no. The reason is that, starting with the ZORK interview, we require them to go a step *beyond* being friendly—We demand that they "WOW" the people at their table with their description of that bottle of wine or bananas foster flambe. So, from the very first time they wear our uniform, they are not only focused on making our guests comfortable, but increasing their sales and ours.

The best servers are those who can "WOW" you with their descriptions of things you've never tried, perhaps even things you never knew existed! The ZORK Interview not only shows us who the best servers are before we hire them, it reinforces a simple truth about salesmanship: if you love people, and you're not afraid of an audience, you'll be a great salesperson--whether you're selling a $4.95 Cherries Jubilee or the $250,000 ZORK.

Fire Them Before You Hire Them

Ray Kroc, the founder of McDonald's, tells this all-too-familiar story of the employee who should have been fired long before he was:

The man hung on. Hew was on the verge of being fired several times in the following years, but he was transferred or got a new supervisor each time. He was a decent guy, so each new boss would struggle to reform him. Many years later he was fired. The assessment of the executive who finally swung the ax was that 'this man has no potential.'

. . .Our expenditure of time and effort on that fellow was wasted, and, worst of all, he spent several years of his life in what turned out to be a blind alley. It would have been far better for his career if he'd been severed early and forced to find work more suited to his talents. It was an unfortunate episode for both parties. . .

Why do we hang onto bad people long after we know they won't make it? Obviously, there are any number of personal reasons (most people don't want to tell someone that they have "no potential"), but the fundamental error is that most of us put the hiring and firing process in the wrong order.

Firing Comes First

Let me give you an example from Old San Francisco. Years ago, we did what most restaurants do in an employee interview—we asked questions that had everything to do with *when* they could work (When are you available? How close do you live? Do you have experience working a bar on a Friday night? and so on), and asked little about *how* they could work. We ended up hiring pulses who we knew we could always fire later—most of the time, we did, after wasting huge amounts of money training them. As much as I would have liked to believe it sometimes, the problem was not that they were bad people, per se; our interview had set them up for failure by defining their principal skills as living nearby and being available for work on Sundays. We knew nothing about their personality, or their motivation level before it was too late.

So we reversed the process. Now when a prospective employee sits down for an interview, we put a bottle of wine and a glass in front of them and tell them to open it and serve a glass properly. If they do it right, we take them to the bar and ask them to make a martini. If they can't do it, we fire them: we say "thank you", and the interview is over. We move on to personality later, asking questions we know they haven't rehearsed in advance. One of my favorites is "What kind of animal would you be and why?" That may sound ridiculous, but, personality-driven questions like this provoke incredibly telling responses. We may, for example, find out that the same bartender applicant who's a great drink mixer is also a "lamb": a meek personality who can't take control.

In the end, we not only hire people with the skill sets and personalities which we need, but we've already fired the ones who aren't cut out to work with us.

Let your competitors waste their time firing people! We've learned that we can't take people from kindergarten to college in our restaurants. We've got to hire the ones who can already WOW our guests by delivering great customer performance.

Grow the Right Carrots

If you take anyone for granted, you'll lose them.

Gordon Bethune, chairman, Continental Airlines

High employee turnover in the hospitality business has become a given. We lose people constantly because they are poorly trained, poorly managed, and, most often, simply ignored.

This last mistake has led most of us to initiate employee recognition plans—such as "employee of the month" certificates—and to teach our managers that the more they praise their employees, the better. However, "high touch" management is less about the *quantity* of positive reinforcement than the *means* of positive reinforcement; in other words, growing the right carrots to motivate employees is the key to retaining them.

Why? Thanks largely to the disappearance of the career path, recognition from someone up the corporate ladder doesn't necessarily provide a perceived benefit. The carrots we use today must have a tangible value to employee and employer alike; they must offer an immediate benefit that is measurable. Moreover, they must be structured in a way which allows the most challenged—or least motivated—employee to succeed.

Starbucks Coffee Co. has become one of the world's most successful growth companies in recent years by providing even its part-time employees—the ones who are so often ignored by the rest of us—with health benefits and stock options. Continental Airlines has become the most successful turnaround story in the airline industry by offering every employee, from its flight mechanics to pilots, substantial cash bonuses based upon the success with which they do their job. Like Starbucks, Continental has increased the quality of its service above that of its competitors by motivating *all* of its people into action.

At Old San Francisco, incentives are a daily part of what we do, and we involve everyone. Here's a few examples:

- **Server Bingo** - Our servers are challenged to sell certain items on our menu by playing "bingo". When they sell a certain item, they fill a space, until someone wins. The reward? Usually lottery tickets, which create a million dollars worth of excitement for two bucks.
- **Dishwasher Awards** - Most executives ignore their dishwashers; after all, they do nothing but clean dishes, right? Wrong. Dishwashers are cost managers. Partnering with AmeriClean, our dishwashing vendor, we together identified our base level of breakage and loss expenditures, then created cash bonuses and award certificates based on breakage and loss reduction. These costs are now down to the lowest levels we've ever experienced, and they'll stay that way.
- **Employee Anniversary Parties** - Recently, a busboy celebrated his fifth anniversary with our company. Big deal? It was for us! Our employees threw him a surprise anniversary party, complete with cake, whistles and party gifts.

It is so easy to forget about people, especially when you assume that they won't be around three months from today. We may not be able to distribute stock options, benefits plans and multi-million dollar bonus pools, like Starbucks and Continental, but we can grow new carrots that reward our employees in a way that's meaningful to them, and to us.

Train the concept, not the details

Too many of us equate our employees with our beloved personal computers: brainless machines who have to be programmed to perform every task down to the most minute detail. I don't know how many times I've seen a chief operations officer pull out his company's voluminous operations manual and proclaim, in a slightly veiled reference to his employees, "this is idiot proof." I guarantee you that it's anything but.

Trying to "program" employees only the details of their jobs—the whos, whats, whens and hows—is a recipe for absolutely terrible service and low morale. Not that detailed training isn't important. It is. But employees first need to be taught the concept: *why* they are doing a particular job. Without knowing the concept, employees have no way of adjusting to particular situations, of coping when the scenario before them isn't picture perfect. And in our business, of course, it rarely is.

Let me give you a trivial, but probably familiar, example. The other day, I ate lunch with a friend at a quick service chain. When we were finished, my friend decided to get a milkshake for the ride home. Placing the order, the cashier, who had served us thirty minutes earlier, looked at him and asked "would you like to try our new double-bacon cheeseburger?"

My friend was dumbfounded. "No," he answered.

Didn't the cashier know that my friend had just eaten? And, after all, didn't she know that the chance he'd want a bacon cheeseburger with his milkshake was abysmally low? Probably. But the restaurant's policies had made his wishes irrelevant. The cashier was doing her job, reading from the suggestive selling script given to her that morning by her manager, who was looking over her shoulder to make sure she followed every detail. The manager was pleased—the employee had done her job. My friend, the customer, was dumbfounded. It didn't make any sense!

I should acknowledge that suggestive selling is one of the most effective ways we boost sales in our businesses. But, when we simply teach the details—what to say, for example—and ignore the individual context, even very effective tools like suggestive selling quickly become self-defeating. Had this chain taught its people the *concept* of suggestive selling instead of (or, at least, in addition to) a script, the cashier might have sold my friend a large instead of a small, or perhaps something for dessert. Instead, she reduced herself—and him—to characters out of a policy manual that was probably written years ago.

What's the problem? Most upper-level managers and entrepreneurs assume that employees already know the concept, so they focus their training on the smallest details. Others, unfortunately, believe that line employees (the "idiots") simply can't be trusted with the idea of "concept" to begin with. Then, of course, these managers become incredibly frustrated when employees do nothing more than the details they've so carefully been ordered to do, so they teach them more details until their operations manual is four inches thick and "idiot proof"! I guess they think that the concepts will somehow filter down by osmosis. But that doesn't work. If you want your people to do the best job that they possibly can, and make your business as successful as possible, you've got to tell them the whys first; then let them frame every detail within the vision of your concept.

The purpose of management is to both train and motivate employees. Yet we, as hospitality providers, are notorious for unmotivated people who leave our companies at every opportunity. Why? The most common complaint is that we simply can't afford to keep employees by paying higher wages and bonuses. But the reality is—when it costs an average of $2,000 to train an employee—none of us can afford 100, 200, even 400%+ turnover! Clearly, the more we motivate our people to stay with us, the more money we *save*, and not vice-versa.

At Old San Francisco, we developed the Self-Directed TEAM, a tool that allows us to pay our people more, keep them longer, and reduces those expensive turnover rates. TEAMs are a "high-touch" way to reward people every day, and, more importantly, to allow people to initiate positive change without the participation of management. A few examples:

RECOGNITION TEAM

There is a saying that no good deed goes unpunished, but our recognition TEAM makes sure that no good deed, however small, goes *unnoticed* by fellow employees. Whether handing out simple "thank-yous" or throwing a surprise "anniversary" party for a long-time employee, our recognition TEAM doesn't let employees slip through the cracks.

BUSINESS DEVELOPMENT TEAM

The task of the Business Development TEAM is to go *outside* of the business to "WOW" customers and potential customers. Although their budget is small, our business development team has made us pretty famous among local businesses, which we visit frequently, free wine and cheese in tow. It's great to "WOW" them in the restaurant, but you've got to have people working on the outside as well, pushing the envelope from the other direction.

CONTEST TEAM

Our Contest TEAM's mandate is to motivate employees on a very tight budget, so the real reward of each contest is the fun and challenge of winning the contest. That means using low-cost incentives, and contests that everyone can understand.

Our Contest TEAM makes contests a team activity as often as possible, pairing up the most and least successful employees for a particular task. This creates an automatic training effect, where the lesser employee learns to come up to the level of the more successful one.

SCHEDULING TEAM

We noticed a long time ago that managers were spending too much valuable time creating schedules that, more often than not, underwent dramatic changes during the week anyway.

Now our scheduling is handled by a TEAM, using a simple grid that determines how many servers, busboys and other employees we need for certain levels of sales. If we project 400 covers, for example, we need twenty servers. All our manager does is forecast daily sales. The scheduling TEAM does the rest.

Just TEAM It!

We also have TEAMs maintaining the appearance of our restaurants, hiring new employees, and doing other important tasks. Organizing people together under a common purpose increases motivation because it makes their jobs far more interesting and fun. Our success in reducing turnover while increasing productivity proves the equation "TEAM=Together Everyone Achieves More."

Create Psychological Ownership

At Old San Francisco, we know that our success ultimately depends on the thousands of small decisions which our employees make each day, not just the several big decisions handled by management. We also realize that, in order for these employees to be truly empowered to make the right decisions, we must provide them with an incentive to do the right thing. In other words, we must provide them with a "buy-in" to their job which empowers them to make a difference, to "WOW" *themselves*. We refer to this "buy-in" as *psychological ownership*: their psychological investment in the business.

How do we give our employees psychological ownership of their jobs? We start by treating them like they'll be around tomorrow, because we want them to stay. We learn about them, and, more importantly, we listen to them. This lets our employees know that, ultimately, we realize ownership of the job is theirs, and not ours.

Let me illustrate the power of psychological ownership with two contrasting examples.

The other day, one of our guests called to compliment us for exceptional service. He had left his wallet in his car, so, after dinner, he left the table and asked a valet to point him towards his car. Instead of giving our guest the keys and, in effect, telling him to fetch his wallet himself, the valet promptly brought the guest's car to the entrance, allowing him to get his wallet without leaving the greeting area. Then our valet re-parked the car near the front of the restaurant, just so our guest would not feel rushed.

That's a lot of effort for no additional tip. Our customer was understandably "WOW"ed.

Now here's a much different example. Not long ago, when I was checking out my rental car at a new airport, the attendant handed me an ice scraper. At first, I was impressed, mistakenly thinking that the scraper was a courtesy for the following morning. When I got to the car, however, the windshield was *already* frozen over. The attendant wasn't anticipating a future need, as I assumed—he was just too lazy to scrape the ice off himself! So I spent the next fifteen minutes scraping ice off of someone else's car in my suit and tie, and reminding myself to banish this company from my rolodex.

Our valet operated differently from the car-rental company's attendant because he possessed some psychological ownership which made him *want* to go the extra distance. Why? For one, he feels responsible for his job. And he knows that his job makes a difference to a lot of people, including me, because I never hesitate to thank him for it when I visit this restaurant. Just as he "WOW"ed our customer that day, I want to "WOW" him with my own appreciation and faith in his ability to do a terrific job.

Invest in Your People

Of course, if this valet thought that the purpose of his job was to park cars, he could have total ownership of his job and still be oblivious to the customer. So we go one step further: we demand that our employees feel psychological ownership of not just their jobs, but of their customer's total experience. This requires a substantial investment on our part, because it means that every employee understands their individual contribution to the overall dining experience, every day. We make this investment in two steps:

1. Create Knowledge

To give employees ownership of the customer experience, they must first possess the knowledge of exactly what that experience is, meaning that everyone in our organization—from the dishwasher on up—has eaten a meal in our dining room. So, instead of thinking of cleaning a bunch of dishes, that employee is thinking about presenting a clean plate in front of the customer. We also make sure that every department has its own vision statement, conceived by that department.

2. Create Cross-Ownership

Because creating a customer experience is a team effort, we also want to make sure that everyone is working together all of the time. At Old San Francisco, we divide ownership for nine tables among teams of three servers (who physically serve only three tables each) and a busboy. Before every shift, each member of the team gives a mental and physical percentage to the other members. So, if one server is only at 50% mentally (perhaps they're under a great deal of personal stress), the other servers know, in advance, that they'll probably own a little more of that server's tables that night. Creating this kind of "cross ownership" creates a safety net for our people, and for our customers. It also ensures that no one in our establishments will ever hear "that's not my table."

W.O.W. 2000

Management Summary & Quick Check-up

Traditional

- Build a Single Career Path For Everyone
- Hire Mercenaries
- Pay Minimum Wage
- Create Voluminous "Ops Manuals"
- Command and Control
- Tell Employees What To Do
- Hire, Then Fire Those Who Don't Work
- Give People Narrowly Defined Tasks

W.O.W. 2000

- Understand Individual Priorities
- Create Employee-Partners
- Use Incentives to Pay People More
- Teach the Concept First
- Allow Employees to Initiate Change
- Listen to Them to Know What To Do
- Don't Hire Those Who Won't Work
- Create Ownership of the Entire Customer Experience for Each Employee

Where You Are Today

- % of Your Employees Who Are:

_____Mercenaries

_____Loyalists

_____Partners

- % of Your Training Which Is:

_____Operational Details

_____% of Your Managers' Time

Spent On:

_____High Pay-Off Activities

_____Non-Essential Tasks

_____Creating Employee Incentives

Where You Want To Be Tomorrow

- % of Your Employees Who Are:

_____Mercenaries

_____Loyalists

_____Partners

- % of Your Training Which Is:

_____Operational Details

_____% of Your Managers' Time

Spent On:

_____High Pay-Off Activities

_____Non-Essential Tasks

_____Creating Employee Incentives

PART III

Towards 2000:
A Whole New World

New Roads

Two roads diverged in a wood and I--

I took the one less traveled by.

And that has made all the difference.

Robert Frost

This has only worked because we dared to do it a lot differently.

Chris Sullivan, co-founder, Outback Steakhouse

The path to success in 1957 is an express lane to failure in 1997. Intuitively, this is hardly a shocking statement. After all, everyone knows that our world has changed dramatically since the 1950s—in terms of diversity, lifestyles, priorities, attitudes, income, and so on. Yet the vast majority of hospitality providers today operate upon the same paradigms which fueled the success of McDonald's forty years ago: consistency, market share and brand awareness.

In other words, while the landscape has changed dramatically, most of us are trying desperately to follow an already well-beaten path to success, a path which offers a proven formula. Few want to risk failure by doing it differently.

But that, ironically, is exactly what we assure if we continue down the well-beaten paths, which are littered with the roadkill of so many McDonald's knock-offs and cookie cutter chains. Companies like Roy Rogers, Discovery Zone, Rally's Drive-In, Rax Restaurants, Sizzler, and China Coast all followed the chain recipe, and all have either declared bankruptcy or disappeared altogether. Companies like Outback Steakhouse, on the other hand, have succeeded precisely because they found another, less-traveled path to follow.

For the past twenty-five years, I have witnessed an incredibly destructive tidal wave of "me-too" concepts descend upon the hospitality industry, creating a supply of similar dining experiences which far outstrips the demand. I have come to realize that, for most of us, changing course offers the only real chance of success; if we do not choose what the eminent poet Robert Frost once termed "the road less traveled", we will surely end up washed away in its path, like the others.

Ever since McDonald's revolutionized hospitality paradigms, our companies have become incredibly proficient at delivering what people expected *yesterday*, not today. As a result, most of us are not focused on delivering what would truly delight and surprise our customers—what we call "WOW" experiences. But delivering these kinds of experiences is the only path to success, as concepts like Rainforest Cafe, Caribou Coffee, Planet Hollywood, Dive!, Outback Steakhouse, and Old San Francisco are proving. The old strategy, which consisted of duplicating the same concept as many times as possible, just doesn't work anymore.

Understanding the Population Metamorphosis

Depending on who's talking, America is either an exploding collage of diverse citizens and lifestyles, or a formerly great nation teetering on moral and financial ruin. The reality lies somewhere in between. Yes, no aspect of our country's population metamorphosis is more obvious than its unprecedented diversity, a diversity which, as Lee Iacocca has remarked, must be its strength and not its weakness. But, we are also a nation burdened by the weight of extraordinary personal and government debts, twin albatrosses which strangle our potential to grow in the 21st century.

One way to understand the population metamorphosis, at least qualitatively, is to turn on the television. The Cleaver family is gone, although not totally forgotten. Today, along with the nostalgic favorites of the fifties (now relegated to their own cable channels), are literally hundreds of shows celebrating, criticizing and analyzing America's various modern subcultures: from our inner cities and suburbs to our new places of work and play. We no longer speak of a single America, but a collection of very different Americas.

What are the general trends?

Although America remains overwhelmingly white (roughly 70%), minorities are on the rise. So are teenagers and college students, who influence spending far more than they ever have before. Not only do these younger groups flex a lot of financial muscle at home, they have more access to credit than ever before. One in every three teenagers now carries their own credit card.

America is becoming older at a rapid pace. Although only one in eight Americans is currently over 65 years of age, that figure will more than double in the next forty years, as the baby boom generation moves into their sixties. The more ominous statistic? The working class will bear the burden of its older generation much more in the future than in the past, as the ratio of working people to retirees falls from 3 to 2.

The rich are getting richer and the poor are getting poorer. The good news is that elderly Americans are now experiencing their lowest poverty rate of the twentieth century. The bad news is that younger Americans are experiencing an unprecedented and stubborn decline below the poverty level. The top 1% of Americans now control more wealth than at any other time in our history, even as roughly one-third of our children live in poor households. Moreover, rich Americans are placing themselves at as great a distance as possible from their poor counterparts, by retreating to the suburbs and building gated communities. Management guru Peter F. Drucker recently called this trend one of the biggest dangers we face heading into the future. I agree.

The labor pool, the reservoir of manpower from which all businesses in America sustain themselves, has become increasingly low-wage and temporary in nature. The primary concerns of hospitality employers have proven to be:

1) a gigantic increase in the proportion of low-wage workers, and

2) a far less equitable distribution of rewards among the participants.

Over the past decade, the number of low-wage workers as defined by the Census (those making less than $12,195 in 1990 dollars) nearly doubled, from 7.8 million to more than 14 million. Roughly one-third of those workers are involved in jobs which they identify as temporary, while the Labor Department recently estimated that an additional 15 million or so are either employed by temporary leasing companies or are working on a temporary basis. The proportion of the workforce which can now be classified as low-wage has increased even more dramatically, and now includes over one-quarter of American workers.

The bright spot? American households have managed to eke out increases in income over the years, by combining more incomes into fewer households. But even with poorer Americans pooling their resources under the same roof, the gap between rich and poor households has continued to grow. The top 20% of American households now boast as much purchasing power as the middle 60%.

Will the current low-wage system continue into the 21st century? Apparently so, largely thanks to hypercompetitive industries with little room for increasing pay (the average restaurant, for example, now achieves a razor thin margin of 4%). So, rather than create a new generation of careers—jobs which offer clear opportunities for advancement and education—American companies are actually moving at a breakneck speed to *eliminate* them in favor of cheaper and more flexible labor. McDonald's and Sears led the way to creating a completely part-time workforce by getting rid of all full-time, non-executive positions. Moreover, many companies continue to reengineer to increase their efficiency, meaning that the 2.3 million middle management jobs eliminated by corporate America over the last five years will probably never re-appear. The temporary, low-wage workforce seems to be the future.

America's largest minority groups. . . .

33,000,000 Black Americans

27,000,000 Hispanic Americans

29,000,000 teens

15,500,000 college students

10-12,500,000 gay Americans

America At Work & At Home. . .

73,000,000 Americans are classified as "white collar"

32,000,000 Americans are classified as "blue collar"

30,000,000 Americans work at home

23,000,000 Americans live alone (300% more than in 1960)

Americans In Their Spare Time. . . .

130,000,000 Americans are coffee drinkers

35,000,000 Americans have used an on-line service in the past 3 months

12,000,000 American households subscribe to an on-line service

5,700,000 Americans read "Cooking Light"

Average household spending on casino gambling: $131

A Few Surprises. . .

12.5% of the population is over 65

28% of churchgoers are over 60

24% of Americans are on a diet

Over 1,000,000 Americans will declare personal bankruptcy this year

$ of Tea Sales in the U.S. (1996): 3,000,000,000

Per Capita Consumption of Red Meat (1995): 122 lbs.

% of Master Cardholders who believe that restaurant dining is a luxury: 60

No. of sub shops in the United States (1996): 17,888

Membership of Burger King's Kid's Club: 6,000,000

Average check size (casual dining): $10.17

Average check size (quick-service): $5.39

No. of North Americans who use the Internet: 30,000,000

America Has Become Bilingual

San Antonio, the city in which Old San Francisco is based and in which I live, has quietly become the tenth largest city in the nation. It is also predominately Hispanic. As a white transplant from New York, I will probably always be a minority here. But among cities in Texas and along the West Coast, San Antonio is not unusual. Visit any region of the Southwest and nearly every sign, ATM, and telephone service will offer an English and Spanish version. These areas have literally become bilingual.

But America has become bilingual in a much more profound sense. Spanish-speaking citizens are, after all, only one minority, and not even the largest. The American socio-economic map is now divided up into a series of overlapping minorities so vast that no one person can possibly remember them all; they take into account everything imaginable, skin color, language, income, gender and age, to name a few.

What does this mean? Essentially that every citizen—every potential customer—is *at least* bilingual. The same person who works at a retail boutique in an exclusive, predominately white neighborhood may live in a less wealthy, predominately black neighborhood. That person may "speak" white upper-class at work, and Ebonics at home. The days when everyone came to work from the same neighborhood and talked about the previous evening's episode of "I Love Lucy" are gone forever. Americans have become adept at adjusting to their surroundings temporarily, not being identified by them. Identity today is, in fact, largely situational. A customer may be one type of person at home, one person at work, and yet another at a nightclub on the weekends.

The reality of a bilingual culture can yield strange, and to some, disturbing results. Consider, for example, that the largest consumers of black "gangsta' rap" music are white, suburban teenagers, while some of the most loyal buyers of Tommy Hilfiger clothes—which are advertised by an almost exclusively white cadre of prep-school attending models—are black teenagers from the inner cities. Neither the white suburbanite or the inner-city black feels any conflict between their buying decisions and the message of their respective suppliers: gangsta' rap artists and preppy clothes manufacturers. In other words, they can be whomever they want to be.

Recently, I was asked to give a speech on business to a group of high-school students. Although I had planned to begin the talk with a discussion of values—integrity, persistence, and so forth—my "value focused" introduction was vetoed by the students' teacher, who suggested that I "cut to the chase." In other words, she wanted me to talk immediately about what the kids wanted to hear: how to make lots of money.

I soon realized why. To these kids, an attention span was something that lasted for no longer than a few minutes, approximately the length of a music video. Furthermore, they did not understand business as an extension of a more personal journey, or even as a means to an end. To this generation, I soon realized, business means making money. And making money means buying things: Air Jordans, BMWs, fancy vacations, you name it.

Twenty years ago, if I'd asked this classroom what they wanted to be, hands would have sprung up. Responses would have included things like "surgeon", "scientist", "astronaut", and so on. But when I posed the familiar question to this classroom, no one said anything. I was shocked! My next question was "how many of you want to make lots of money?" All of the hands shot up. "Well," I said, "How do you plan to make lots of money?" The hands all went down. Nobody knew. To be honest, nobody cared. All they know is that they want to be "rich"—a brand if their ever was one.

As marketers, we deserve much of the blame for the current values system. We've become so skilled at telling young people what they want, and attaching a brand name to it, that we have neglected to teach them an important lesson: success is a by-product of hard work, ingenuity and persistence, not a destination to reach as quickly as possible.

We should also understand that all of our whiz-bang technology and hip video artistry has created a generation with an infinitesimal attention span. Our television shows, movies and music videos have conditioned them to stay focused on one particular subject for no more than five seconds, the length of a camera shot in an action movie.

In other words, all of our savvy marketing has had a profound impact on values; it has reared an incredibly brand-conscious, wealth-obsessed and technology-hungry generation of consumers. It has made our children care far more about what they drive and wear than what impact they have on society as a whole. Of course, there are encouraging signs that many of us have become disenchanted (or perhaps just bored) with all of the flash, but it will probably take decades for substance to be trendy again.

Understanding the Lifestyle Metamorphosis

Although the diversity of today's population makes it difficult to talk about a single lifestyle metamorphosis, we can identify a few common denominators:

The Two Wage-Earner Family The emergence of the two-wage earner family model to replace the traditional one wage-earner has produced by far the most profound lifestyle shifts.

First off, the emergence of the two wage-earner family means that, with nearly all of us are participating in the workforce, few people have much time to spare. Is it any wonder that a recent survey found that 80% of Americans demand speedy service wherever we do business, and that 75% of eating decisions are made within 5 minutes of purchase? In fact, every major fast-food chain now does as much or more business in the single drive-through lane outside than in the entire dining room inside.

The two wage-earner household has also dramatically shifted the places where we purchase food. There are now three times as many restaurants as grocery stores; cooking is thought of as more of a luxury than a necessity. Who has the time?

Finally, with no time and tight budgets, people are turning to simple pleasures to provide some respite from the hectic schedules and stress. That's why quick indulgences like massages and super-premium ice cream have become such big sellers.

Households are Getting Larger Today, one in every four middle-aged households includes at least one adult who is still living at home. More people are living under the same roof primarily because it makes economic sense, although many households are composed of "hybrid" families as well; these are the families formed when two divorced or widowed people re-marry and combine their households into one.

We're Living Scared Despite the fact that crime has decreased steadily for the past several years, people are more scared than ever. Home alarm systems, car alarms and gated communities are all growth industries, fueled by sensationalist news reports and racial tensions which, as the O.J. Simpson trial showed, have proven stubborn.

We're Paying Later American consumers have now amassed a collective $1 trillion-plus of installment debt (credit cards, auto leases, and so on.). Everything we own, from our homes to our vacations, can now be financed; moreover, delayed payment terms e.g. "No payments until next year!", have become an integral part of any product and its advertising. The resulting pile of debt has created a surge in personal bankruptcies (which will top 1 million this year), as well as new trends like "house-poor" communities--areas which appear affluent, but which boast little disposable income because residents are living so tightly within their means.

Faith Popcorn Was Right

When did we start becoming so scared? A long time ago, actually.

In the 1970s, Faith Popcorn and her small army of social scientists at BrainReserve predicted that Americans would begin "cocooning", a phenomenon which she defined as "the impulse to go inside when it just gets too tough and scary outside. To pull a shell of safety around yourself, so you're not at the mercy of a mean, unpredictable world."

Faith Popcorn was right.

Today, 52.5% of Americans shop at home, tens of millions work from their home "cocoons", and the average American watches 54 hours of home videos per year, up 55% from 1988. Moreover, corporate headquarters has shifted from space in a downtown skyscraper to the " corporate campus"—a self-sufficient community where employees can enter and literally never leave, protected by gates, and constantly patrolled by company security. The most successful new product introduction in recent memory was the mini-satellite dish, a piece of wizardry that allows homeowners to view no less than 500 channels of programming. Soon, we won't even have to go to the video store to rent our favorite movie. Already, software is allowing us to forego the traditional jaunt to the bank (electronic banking), the post office (e-mail), and even the grocery store (home delivery via Web page).

Even when we are on the road today, we re-create our home and office cocoons. Hence what I call the "urban assault vehicle"—the four-wheel drive monster truck decked out with fog lamps, huge bumpers, protective grids around the lights, tinted windows and cellular phones, to name a few options. I'm not sure if anyone actually uses the four-wheel drive, much less the fog lamps or automotive riot gear, at least where I live. But it makes them feel safe. I should know—I just bought one for my wife!

Popcorn's observations have played out in the customer-service arena as well; today's retailers re-create home cocoons by designing "cocoon-like" environments where their customers will feel both comfortable and secure. When I go to the grocery store today, there's at least one policeman by the door; when I go to the shopping mall, I can have my car valet parked, so I don't have to risk a car-jacking; and if I pay the premium for first-class on some overseas flights, I'm even provided a seat with temporary walls which surround me and create my own personal cocoon aboard the aircraft. In the twenty years since Faith Popcorn first observed cocooning, that "shell of safety" has become a fact of life for most of us, and those of us who can are more than willing to pay for it.

Faith Popcorn Was Wrong

Now a caveat.

What Faith Popcorn neglected to realize is that cocoons are, by definition, temporary places. While it is natural to shelter ourselves when we feel that the outside world is scary, we don't withdraw from it entirely. We cannot.

Our most personal challenge is to *emerge* from our cocoons successfully: from fearful caterpillars to resilient butterflies. The transition—which allows us to be "high touch" with everyone around us—is always filled with angst, pain and doubt. Few of us can accomplish it without help, especially if we have grown up in an affluent, protective environment where we've always felt warm and safe.

When I was growing up, leaving the cocoon was far easier. In fact, I now realize that I learned how to become "high touch" very early simply because I *had* to. There was no Nintendo 64, satellite television or VCR. If I wanted to be entertained, I had to seek out the neighbors and we created the games ourselves (stickball was a favorite). When I left for college, I packed my bags, kissed my parents goodbye, and rarely looked back (sorry, Mom and Dad—I still don't nearly as much as I should).

Today, parents seem to have adapted a much different philosophy. They follow their children to school, bearing all the comforts of home, with which they create a "college" cocoon. Then they give their "kids" a calling card, just in case anything "happens." Is it any wonder that 25% of 30-year-olds still live at home? As a woman with two college-aged children recently confided to me "I used to worry about taking care of my parents in their old age. Now I'm worried that we'll have to build an addition to our home to accommodate our children."

But just because we've made our cocoons more comfortable doesn't mean that we'll stay there forever. Cocoons are places where people retreat, to emerge and reemerge at will. Indeed, one of the major lifestyle trends today is a return to "town centers": urban environments with retail, residential and business zones. People are crowding coffee houses as never before to socialize. And high-energy restaurants are doing a booming business, as people seek "eatertainment" out among the living.

In fact, with so many businesses focused on eliminating the human element (you can now order groceries over the Internet, or get a hamburger and fries from a vending machine) people are literally starved for "high touch" experiences. Look at the success of mega-malls and mega-plexes (giant movie theaters with enclosed restaurants). When people leave their cocoons, they want to be "WOW"ed, not just entertained; if they simply wanted to go shopping or see a movie, any number of catalogues and television channels would save them the trip to the outside world.

At Old San Francisco, we recognized the skyrocketing demand for high-touch years ago, and it influences everything we do: how we treat our customers, our employees, our vendors, and our communities. For example, one of our most effective promotions is to send chefs and waitstaff on "wine and cheese runs". These spontaneous promotions consist of a vanload of our people visiting a service establishment—a hair salon, for example—and serving them wine and cheese on the spot. It's the kind of connection which businesses rarely make with customers anymore, and it works better than any advertising we've ever done.

It is also proactive, in the sense that we are encouraging potential customers to come out of their own cocoons, if only for the few hours which they spend with us. Catching butterflies has indeed become more difficult today; we need to not only be there when customers emerge, however late in life, but we also need to WOW them out of their sophisticated and comfortable shells.

PART IV

The New Financial Challenge:
Create a Profitable Concept

The Power of the Compound Return

Charlie Munger, the man who helped Warren Buffett turn Berkshire Hawathay from a fledgling mill into one of the largest conglomerates in the world, recently told *Fortune* magazine the secret of his investing success: **the power of the compound return**. It is also the secret to success in the hospitality business.

Simply put, the power of the compound return is released when positive results are achieved year after year after year. As the enterprise grows, consistently positive returns create a snowball effect; before long, what began as a small series of achievements has become a monumental success.

Of course, compounding is most often associated with passive investments. But success in the restaurant industry is also the result of compounding: day after day, month after month, and year after year, customers are gained. Word-of-mouth and solid advertising capitalize on the previous year's gain. Solid operations and constant innovation protect the business' foundation. In other words, a restaurant increases the value of its "investment"—its loyal core of customers—by retaining existing ones first and consistently gaining new ones every year. Consider: if a restaurant began with one-thousand regular customers, and was able to attract just five new customers per week, losing 1% or so each year due to death or moving, within five years it will count close to 2,500 regular customers; within ten years, the number increases to just under 6,200. Not bad.

Of course, that's assuming that no customers are lost. And that, as Munger knows, is the real secret of the power of compounding: never, ever lose money. Or, in the restaurant's case: *never, ever lose a regular customer.* Can we bring in five new customers a week? As a marketer, I can say that's easy. Word-of-mouth alone can accomplish that. Where do we fail? Retaining customers, protecting that base that produces the real gains.

A recent study published in the *Harvard Business Review* sheds new light on why customers leave. It's not because the ads aren't good enough; and it's not because of aggressive new competitors. The top three reasons which researcher Susan M. Keaveney found were as follows:

1. *Core-service failures* Simple mistakes, billing errors and what Keaveney referred to as "service catastrophes" are the three top reasons why customers leave and never come back. In fact, 44% of former customers cited these mistakes as reasons for leaving, a statistic which makes training seem cheap. Yet how many of us take the time to teach an employee the proper way to serve a bottle of wine?

2. *Service encounter failures* What Keaveney describes as "failures in the personal interactions between customers and employees", these include uncaring, impolite, unresponsive or unknowledgeable employees. No wonder Starbucks and the Boston Beer Company, which both screen employees extensively, have gained such loyal followings.

3. *Price* Because customers are literally bombarded with restaurant prices now—on storefronts, in newspapers, direct mail, and even television ads—most have specific expectations of price. If you're charging more than what they expect, they'll disappear.

Inconvenience and *employees' responses when service failed* rounded out the top five.

Interestingly, slightly more than half (55%) of departing customers in Keaveney's study cited more than one disappointment, meaning that most customers give an establishment a second chance. But when customers finally leave, it's usually with a vengeance: they are ten times as likely to tell friends about their bad experience than complain directly to the business owner or manager.

For investors, gaining the power of the compound return requires patience, innovation, but most importantly, discipline. The same is true of restaurant operators. In order to move successfully forward, marketing efforts may be modest in scope, but they must be unerringly consistent in execution.

Go For The Obvious

Serve the hot food hot and the cold food cold.

That's the big secret to success in this industry.

Tilman Fertitta, chairman, Landry's Seafood Restaurants

The hospitality industry may be tough, but it's also simple. Becoming profitable requires nothing more than knowing where the profitable opportunities are, then pursuing them. Before we act, however, we've got to allow these opportunities to become obvious by acquiring some simple answers: what do our customers want? What can we deliver that our competitors cannot? What kind of additional services can we provide to be profitable? And so forth. Once we know the answers to these questions, the profitable opportunities become impossible to ignore. At Old San Francisco, we call these opportunities the "cash cows sitting right under our noses", because we always find them grazing in our dining room.

Take a moment to visualize your dining room (or your primary place of business) as a pasture. What opportunities do you see? What cash cows can you "brand" and make your own?

Time *is* Money: high pay-off activities

Remember that time is money.

Benjamin Franklin

If you had more time, could you make more money? The answer for most of us is a resounding "Yes!", yet we often make our time remarkably *unprofitable* by investing it foolishly: fighting fires and confronting the crisis of the moment rather than thinking about how we can increase profits with a terrific new menu item or promotion. So how do we begin to free up our time for making more money? We start by identifying our **high pay-off activities** and **non-essential tasks**.

Simply put, high pay-offs are activities which make us money, better our businesses, increase how many customers we're going bring into our establishment today, or assure that we stay in business by creating loyalty. We also call them "WOW" activities, because they should generate excitement among our customers, our employees, or both. A terrific example of a high pay-off activity is a frequent diner program which we recently rolled out at our restaurants. This program rewards our customers for dining with us more often (by giving them a gift certificate for each $150 they spend with us), and it provides cash incentives for our waitstaff to enroll customers into the program. The payoff? An increase in customer loyalty as well as employee motivation.

Non-essential tasks, on the other hand, are those which can be delegated without losing any customers or potential business. Generally, non-essential tasks are daily routines, like scheduling and dining room checks. They may be very important, but non-essential tasks are always functions of consistency, not innovation.

Today, no restaurateur can afford *not* to innovate. According to the latest figures, fully 60% of restaurants fail within five years, and one in four don't even make it to their first anniversary. If you're not making your time pay off, you can almost count on being in that first 60%.

Where, exactly, do you begin to re-invest your time? Following is a starter of high-pay off and non-essential activities. Spend more time on the former, and delegate the latter. Don't be surprised if you "WOW" yourself with the time you create for new ideas.

High Pay Off (Do it Yourself)

Bring In New Customers

Organize/Energize Employees

Sponsor a New Charitable Event

in the Community

_____

_____

_____

_____

_____

_____

_____

_____

_____

_____

_____

_____

_____

_____

Non-Essential (Delegate)

Scheduling

Create Day-to-Day Contests

Check the Dining Room

Most Employee Hiring

_____

_____

_____

_____

_____

_____

_____

_____

_____

_____

_____

_____

_____

_____

Hire People Who Can Do What You Can't

The other day, I had the opportunity to meet with a twenty-nine year-old entrepreneur, a man who has built a successful regional chain of quick-service restaurants within the space of three years. This venture was his first foray into the restaurant business, and he came to me for some general observations. When I related the details of my disappointing experience at one of his stores, he shook his head knowingly. "I spend 95% of my time building this business," he said, "I don't have time to create the operational systems we need, and none of my business partners have any real experience in restaurants." The systems, therefore, would have to wait. Or so he thought.

I told him that there was one problem with this scenario: customers won't wait. In fact, his customers, employees and franchisees will disappear quickly if long waits and confused orders are allowed to continue at his businesses.

Managers and entrepreneurs often neglect to see the other side of the equation when it comes to issues they have yet to resolve. All they know is that they don't have the time or the experience to do something if it does not relate to the expansion of their enterprise, even if that something is the golden egg which will save, or dramatically enhance, their existing success. So they let service and quality suffer, while their stress level heads into the stratosphere.

Here's a very simple principle: ***you don't have to do it all, but it all has to get done***. In other words, you may not have the time or the expertise to handle a particular task, but that doesn't mean that it can wait until you do. That's why hiring people who can do the things which you can't is so essential.

Moreover, hiring complementary people usually requires no more cost or time. This young entrepreneur, for example, maintains an office staff of five people. He has told me that none of them has any experience in the restaurant industry, so, by definition, there's probably a great deal of duplication in the experiences which they share. Even though it will be painful to bring in new people—and part with the old—he needs to eliminate this duplication and create synergy instead.

But currently, he's trying to teach the franchise director about franchising, the operations guy about running stores and the bookkeeper about accounting. Not only are important things going undone (which he knows), but there is no consistent effort being expended in critical areas which affect the customers' experience; in other words, "E=MC^2" is producing a fraction of its potential.

Don't Build a House of Cards

It took approximately two years for the largest real estate dynasty in the world to crumble. In 1993, the Reichman family—whose net worth had been estimated at $10 billion just two years before—declared bankruptcy, wiping out nearly everything they owned. The problem? What was an admittedly impressive collection of properties—One Canadian Place (the tallest office building in Canada) and the World Trade Center (home of American Express), among others—had been structured as the financial equivalent of a house of cards. Through a series of cross-guarantees, mortgages and financing arrangements, the Reichmann's total wealth was positioned to collapse if a single project failed. Which is exactly what happened.

In the retail/restaurant business, such failures are not uncommon; after all, the losses of a single poorly performing unit can easily wipe out the earnings of several profitable ones. This is probably the single most common reason why young, growing chains suddenly disappear. Their owners become a little cocky with the first or second success, then they overextend their reach with an underperforming unit, and this single mistake takes the entire company into bankruptcy. More often than not, this cockiness is a result of wishful thinking and a mistaken, if prevalent, belief: that more units will mean more success. What is so often forgotten is that for every Starbucks there are dozens of failures which grow too quickly and collapse.

Let me give you an example. Five short years ago, Discovery Zone was riding the crest of a wave. The chain of family recreation centers was entering new markets, building new stores, and acquiring competitors, including Leaps & Bounds, a chain begun by McDonald's. Forcing the burger Goliath to sell to the entertainment David, rather than vice-versa, was regarded as a real coup, and Wall Street responded by pushing Discovery Zone's stock price higher and higher. At its peak, Discovery Zone was a near billion dollar enterprise, selling at an unprecedented P/E ratio of 350.

Then it crashed. Last year, McDonald's wrote off all of its Discovery Zone stock (which it had accepted as payment for Leaps & Bounds) to zero. Why? Discovery Zone had posted a string of gigantic losses and put its very survival as a company in jeopardy. Finally, a small investor in Chicago purchased the beleaguered chain for less than a million dollars total.

What happened? Discovery Zone was structured as a house of cards: the stability of all of the stores rested on the ability of the others to remain upright. Moreover, the Company was counting on all sorts of systemwide marketing programs to make the stores profitable. They were building stores they knew wouldn't be profitable with the expectation that they *would* work once the chain was a big, national name. What they neglected to realize is that foundations become harder, not easier, to build the larger your structure becomes. The time to build the foundation is in the beginning.

W.O.W. Price Points

The customer isn't a moron. She's your wife.

David Ogilvy

Advertising legend David Ogilvy said these words decades ago. And what wasn't true then definitely isn't true now. Customers are smarter than ever: less easily manipulated and more focused on finding real value.

One of the carryovers from the 1950s which assumes the opposite—that customers can't so much as add—are price points. Traditional price points are positioned directly below a new dollar level—say $3.99 rather than $4.00, or $9.95 rather than $10.00—because customers aren't supposed to know the difference. They're supposed to think that $3.99 equals $3.00, not $4.00. But my experience is that today's customers generally know better. Price points don't fool anyone; they lock us in to prices which are arbitrary and unprofitable, forcing us to adjust our quality and portions around pennies on the dollar, not vice-versa.

Several years ago, I began to notice that a few of the most successful restaurants I knew had rejected the traditional price point. Instead of $9.95, for example, an item might be $10.14. When I asked the owners of one of these restaurants how he'd come up with such "weird" prices, he replied that he had been forced to raise prices by 2% the previous year, due to higher food costs. So that's exactly what he did—he got out his calculator and increased every menu item by 2%. His costs stayed exactly in line, and his customers loved it because the pricing changes were completely on-the-level. Imagine—making customers happy by *increasing* prices!

We began instituting "WOW" price points at Old San Francisco recently, and the response has been terrific. One of the first menus we changed was our wine list, which we decided to price at 10% above cost. At first, a few customers expressed surprise, but when we told them why the decimal points ran the gamut, they were really impressed. They knew that we were delivering value, which is exactly what we receive in return.

W.O.W. Relationships are based on three simple principles: mutual benefit, respect and long-term.

Mutual Benefit

No lasting relationship exists for the benefit of one party at the expense of the other. Moreover, both parties should explicitly understand *why* the relationship is mutually beneficial.

Respect

If you don't respect your partners, your relationships will be dysfunctional in the extreme. Managers who show little or no respect to employees can expect their employees to respond in kind.

Long Term

All of your relationships won't last forever, but you should treat them as if they will. It's simply impossible to guess which will endure, which won't, and which you will absolutely depend on for your success down the road. Understanding that your relationships will be around tomorrow fosters trust, mutual respect and understanding. It also means that your partners—be they employees, suppliers or customers—will be far more willing to invest their time (and even money) in your business, because they know that they'll get it back down the road. Plenty of businesses would not be around today had the founders not convinced suppliers and employees that their company was worthy of such trust; no business would be around today without the trust of its customers.

If you've been in business for any length of time, one of the best measures of your success is to take stock of your relationships: are they built on these principles, or are they short-term and apathetic, or, worse, antagonistic? Have you surrounded yourself with people and companies that are more successful than you? Or have you surrounded yourself with the bottom of the barrel—suppliers with few other clients and employees who jump from job to job?

We look at all of our relationships as "high touch" investments, whose potential dividends are immeasurable. Last year alone, our relationships with local businesses produced the following unexpected benefits:

- Samsung, one of the largest electronics firms in the world, included a huge logo and map to one of our restaurants in a full-page ad in our local paper, as part of a map to their new factory.
- A single car dealership bought gift certificates from us to use as new customer incentives, then advertised them, with our logo, on four full-page newspaper ads worth $12,000 apiece.
- AmeriClean, our sanitation vendor, is sponsoring a booth, which will include our Company, at the National Restaurant Association Convention, giving Old San Francisco exposure to hundreds of thousands of food-savvy businesspeople, while AmeriClean provides its customers exposure to the helpful concepts in this book.

As I mentioned, these were unexpected benefits, but they were not surprising. You can bet that we will continue to invest in these, and other relationships, today and that we will reap the benefits tomorrow.

WHY DID SAMSUNG CROSS THE ROAD?

. . .The full-page advertisement which Samsung ran of our restaurant in Austin. Our cost? Nothing. . .

Establish W.O.W. Relationships

Vendors

Yesterday, we were only interested in two things from our vendors: quality and price. Today, we are far more interested in acquiring a strategic partner who will be with us every step of the road ahead. In other words, we are looking for a partner capable of adding to our success, not just a supplier.

At many companies, vendor relationships have become a major selling point. Starbucks, for example, advertises its relationships with its coffee growers on its coffee cups, the Body Shop publishes brochures detailing its involvement with suppliers from poorer countries, Ben & Jerry's reminds people that it is paying its Vermont farmers above-market prices for milk to support the family farm, and so on.

At Old San Francisco, we involve our suppliers in many ways. One of our major sources of competitive advantage today is that we serve 100% Angus Beef. Not only does this commitment differentiate us from our competitors, but it gives me a chance to really get to know our major product supplier. For example, I recently spent several days with the Angus Beef Council, eventually speaking before their annual convention. Every year, I take this time out to learn about Angus Beef, and they have a chance to learn about my restaurants.

But even relationships which don't offer much selling opportunity are worth turning into WOW relationships. Our cleaning supplies vendor, AmeriClean, for example, has become a major partner in cutting costs and making our operations far more affordable. Even though they happen to have thousands of customers, their chief executive officer recently flew to Dallas to listen to my concerns, and tell me how much they appreciate our business. This convinced me that we'd think very long and hard about ever changing cleaning suppliers, and the relationship keeps getting better for both of us.

Of course, there are plenty of executives who still treat their vendors as opponents: they switch from one to another on a weekly basis, depending on price, and train their managers to treat the delivery people as if they were criminals—browbeating them as they meticulously check each delivery for accuracy. Not surprisingly, these vendors tend to treat their clients ·in kind—as adversaries in a price war. In fact, a great deal of the competitive "research" we gain comes directly from delivery people who service our competitors' restaurants as well as ours, because our "high touch" attitude has fostered trust between employees of both companies.

Obviously, W.O.W. relationships do not happen overnight, but they'll never happen if price is the only issue. W.O.W. them with your commitment to be profitable partners, and they'll respond in kind.

Establish W.O.W. Relationships

Customers

The nature of the customer relationship has changed little over the years; what has changed dramatically is the scope of the relationship. In order to create a W.O.W. relationship with our customers, we must touch them *outside* of our places of business.

Let me give you one example. Not long ago, a number of teenagers from the San Antonio area were promised jobs at the Summer Olympics in Atlanta. The only catch was that they had to provide their own transportation. So off they went, many spending their savings on the one-way plane ticket or bus fare. The only trouble was that, once they arrived in Atlanta, there were no jobs. And since many of the teens had expected the Olympics to provide housing, and their wages to pay for the trip home, they were completely stranded.

The story was an outrage, and it made the evening news. It also created a huge opportunity for a local business to come to the community's rescue. Which is exactly what we did. One of our company's owners arranged for Continental Airlines to bring these stranded kids back home, and we hosted a big party at Old San Francisco. The local chapter of the American Heart Association even got involved; they created special "Heart" awards recognizing the wonderful spirit that these kids showed. Our party made the news because the community wanted it to happen, and it generated an inestimable amount of goodwill and publicity. The total cost? Less than one large newspaper ad.

Now, this effort does not fall under the traditional definition of customer service—it goes far beyond it. Reaching out to customers in the communities in which they live, and coming to the their aid in times of need creates a far stronger bond than we could ever hope to accomplish by virtue of excellent service and food alone.

A few favorite examples of W.O.W. customer relationship building at other establishments:

- The chef/owner of an upscale restaurant in Boston has modified his P.O.S. system to recognize the names of frequent customers, as well as their favorite drinks. Now when these customers arrive for dinner, their favorite drink is already waiting at the table.
- A chain of bagel bakeries in the Southwest bought two special tents, and participates in over fifty community events each year, such as races, marathons and golf tournaments. Participants and spectators get free bagels, and this Company gets to know 250,000 potential customers up close.
- A chain of coffee cafes in the Northeast bases its success on employees' abilities to know its customers' favorite espresso drinks within their first three visits. The customers feel special, the line moves faster, and employees can establish relationships instead of just taking orders.

Establish W.O.W. Relationships

Competitors: Stop Benchmarking

Everyone is familiar with the father whose son gets beaten up in a fight, only to exclaim proudly to his neighbors: "you should see the other guy." In business, we call this behavior benchmarking, and it leaves us just about as successful as the kid with two black eyes and a broken nose.

In the restaurant business, benchmarking has accomplished two things: it has made most concepts indistinguishable from one another, and it has provided a convenient excuse for executives to accept poor performance. I can't count the number of annual reports I've read that essentially say: "Yes, we did terribly and lost money. But it's a tough environment and you should feel lucky that you weren't holding stock in some other company, which did *really* badly." I always wonder how everyone can be doing better than everyone else. The truth, of course, is that they aren't. As Warren Buffet likes to say, "if you don't know who the patsy is, it's you."

At Old San Francisco, we use benchmarking once a year, to tell our investors how well we did. That's it. We don't measure ourselves up to them constantly; we don't try to be like them; we don't pretend that they know something which we don't. If we did, our restaurants would be far less successful—we would never have added 100% Angus Beef to our menu, for example, or developed a special, early afternoon New Year's celebration for senior citizens who didn't want to drive home in the dark.

The truth is, our average unit sales are higher than any of our national competitors because we listen to our customers; we don't look to our competitors for a panacea or an excuse.

Not that we don't have anything to learn from our competitors. Quite the contrary. We just don't want to be limited by their vision. We want to W.O.W. them with ours.

For example, when we noticed that some upscale steakhouses were broadening their wine selections, we saw a much larger opportunity to reach out to wine lovers who weren't patronizing our restaurants already. So we teamed up with a popular wine retailer, and hosted wine tastings for their best customers at our restaurant. In our smallest market, these wine tastings are now bringing over 100 new customers into our restaurant every week—of course, we invite them to stay for dinner after the tasting, and many of them do.

Establish W.O.W. Relationships

Employees

Employee relationships drive the success of your business. It's essential that employees can relate positively to you, and you to them.

The old paradigm said that rules and policies were more important than people: if someone deviated from the policy, they must not be a "team" player.

The new paradigm is just the opposite: people are more important than policies—if the policies are making our people miserable, it's probably time we changed the policies, and not vice-versa.

Let me give you one example. We have a policy at Old San Francisco that all employees work every major holiday. Our restaurants are open 365 days a year, and major holidays are very big days for us; in fact, we normally end up hiring extra people for our Thanksgiving and Christmas Day dinners. Last year, a server told us that she had been asked to be in her best friend's wedding as a bridesmaid. This server had been with us over five years, and knew our policy. She also knew that all of the store managers and myself would be working on Christmas Day, the day of the wedding. Therefore, even though she let her co-workers know about the disappointment, she didn't ask for an exception; instead, she assumed, she would just miss the wedding.

When one of our managers learned of her conflict, he basically ordered her to take the day off—he told her that we'd find someone to cover the shift. She was very grateful, and we were sincerely happy for her.

At most companies, a lower-level employee's request for an exception would be met with disapproval at best, and probably a flat "no". After all, once you bend the rules for one person, you've got to break them for everyone. At least, that's big company reasoning.

Our approach is more supportive. The personal lives of our employees, inasmuch as they want to share with us, are indeed our concern. We're interested in them, and we expect them to be interested in the company as a whole. If they're ill, we'll understand and do all that we can to help. If they need a little extra effort from us, we'll try and accommodate. Moreover, if we can't accommodate, we expect them to understand that we tried our best. We want them to come to work feeling happy to be among friends, not miserable among policy enforcers.

One of the best things that we do is provide the resources for our employees to recognize each other's achievements. In an industry where most employees don't last three months, we think that an employee's one-year anniversary is cause for celebration, so their fellow employees throw them a party on their big day, courtesy of Old San Francisco. A five-year anniversary is even better, and we have plenty.

Our old ways assumed that people had little need for affection and "high touch"—that was something which they got at home, from their real families. But we know that this is simply no longer the case for a great many people. We need to provide that support in the workplace by developing much stronger relationships than we have in the past, and that requires mutual commitment.

Just as you focus on increasing today's sales, you should be constantly increasing sales *tomorrow*: guaranteeing a return visit from your current customer, and generating positive word of mouth. When you can be confident that customers will not only return, but tell their friends and acquaintances positive things about your company, the path ahead becomes very clear indeed: a solid sales base, and a never-ending stream of new faces in the door.

At Old San Francisco, we are nothing short of paranoid about generating positive word of mouth, which our employees know as "PWOM". No matter how busy the restaurants, our staff makes sure that every single customer feels like they're the most important person in the place. If a negative experience does occur, we quickly turn it into a positive. For example, if a table is forced to wait longer than usual for their meals, our waitstaff and managers are trained to throw a tableside "wait party"—complete with complementary wine and hors d'oeuvres—to ensure that these customers leave happy and, as we say, "WOW"ed. If we waited for those customers to complain, our sales that night might not be any different, but tomorrow's sales would suffer.

Tilman Fertitta, chairman of Landry's Seafood Restaurants, likes to state: "there are no spare customers." Consider not only that 20% of your customers account for 80% of your business, but that *20% of your customers probably account for 95% of all of our new business,* and you understand that Fertitta's point is probably an understatement. In other words, return customers are not only your overwhelming source of profits today, but by far the most effective generators of new business for tomorrow.

Our mantra at Old San Francisco is "If they love us when they leave us, they'll be back." We know tomorrow's sales by using our old equation "E=MC^2"—as long as we're putting forth the effort, PWOM will deliver the sales.

Don't Be a Spreadsheet Warrior

In the past fifteen years, I've worked for a number of spreadsheet warriors—managers whose primary concern is fitting the company's data as neatly as possible into a pre-ordained set of spreadsheet figures. To them, employees become "labor cost", quality becomes "food cost", maintaining the restaurant's environment becomes "maintenance cost", and so on.

I remember one of these spreadsheet warriors, the c.e.o. of a group of high-volume full-service restaurants, particularly well. As his c.o.o., my job was to eliminate any deviation from "actual" costs (what mattered) to "ideal" costs (what he thought mattered) on his income statements. In other words, my job was not to motivate my employees and to W.O.W. my customers, but to match two sets of numbers in his computer program.

I'm not sure how many arguments we had before I realized that his spreadsheet and my reality would never reconcile. The problem wasn't my lack of commitment to his numbers, but his refusal to learn anything about his restaurants. He didn't know, for example, what it meant for managers to spend three days of the month inventorying smallwares (as his spreadsheet required) rather than building the business. It was incredibly frustrating, because no matter how impressively my managers grew sales and profits, we were never the "ideal". Eventually, I left, and became c.e.o. of Old San Francisco, where I spend most of my time working with managers in the restaurants. It's just as important that I know where the numbers came from as what they happen to be at the end of the day.

There are countless spreadsheet warriors out there. I have seen plenty of franchised systems where the burden of so-called "controls" has become so great that unit-level managers could probably spend every waking hour creating data for corporate. Ironically, as spreadsheet warriors become more and more out of touch with the business itself, they ultimately lose any control of their management, and their precious computer-generated statements end up filled with red ink, or worse, inaccuracies entered by frustrated employees who just feed them the numbers they want to see, regardless of "actual". As techies are so fond of saying "garbage in, garbage out."

W.O.W. 2000

Profitability Summary & Quick Check-up

Traditional

- Advertise for New Customers
- Do What Your Competitors Do
- Give Managers Administrative Duties
- Treat Vendors as Price Opponents
- Be Concerned With Today's Sales
- Treat Employees as "Labor Cost"
- Hire People With Similar Skills
- Manage By Comparing Ideal Numbers To Actual
- Give Customers What They Expect

W.O.W. 2000

- Retain Your Existing Customers
- Find Your Own Cash Cows
- Focus Managers on "High Pay-Off's"
- Treat Vendors as Partners
- Know Tomorrow's Sales Today
- Treat Employees as Cost Managers
- Hire People Who Can Complement You
- Manage By Understanding Where Each Actual Number Came From
- Re-define Your Customers' Expectations with W.O.W. Experiences

Where You Are Today

- % of Sales Which Is:

_____Net Income

_____Advertising

- What are your 3 best-selling items?

_____

_____

_____

- % of Your Customers Who:

_____Patronize you at least 4 times/yr.

_____Spread positive word of mouth

_____Give you positive feedback

Where You Want To Be Tomorrow

- % of Sales Which Is:

_____Net Income

_____Creating/Keeping Loyal Guests

- What are 3 potential "cash-cows"?

_____

_____

_____

- % of Your Customers Who:

_____Patronize you at least 4 times/yr.

_____Spread positive word of mouth

_____Give you positive feedback

PART V

W.O.W. Pioneers:

Starbucks Coffee
Lettuce Entertain You Enterprises
Uncle Julio's Corporation
Caribou Coffee
La Madeleine

Management

Starbucks Coffee Company: CAREing for Employees and Communities

Seattle-based Starbucks Coffee was founded in 1971 by a group of local coffee lovers. Eventually, marketing director Howard Schultz bought out the retail division of the small, but growing, coffee roaster, and began expanding it across the West Coast, modeling the Company's coffee shops on espresso cafes in Milan, Italy. In the past several years, Starbucks has grown from less than 200 stores to well over 1,000.

What's truly impressive about Starbucks, however, is not their growth but the W.O.W. relationships they have established with employees and suppliers. Even part-time employees receive health benefits, most employees receive stock options (called Bean Stock), and the company is the major force behind CARE, an organization which helps to educate children in the poor communities where most of Starbucks' coffees are grown. The result? A committed workforce, the lowest turnover of any major foodservice chain, legendary customer performance, and a limitless supply of the world's best coffee beans.

Financial

Lettuce Entertain You Enterprises: Creating Profits Through Partnerships

Lettuce Entertain You Enterprises is one of the most unique companies on the planet; it is also one of the most successful.

Known as LEYE, the Company was founded twenty-five years ago by Rich Melman, an aspiring entrepreneur who has thrived by helping others to succeed. Along the way, he has created some of the country's most famous restaurants. His stable currently boasts over 40 concepts, including the acclaimed Chicago restaurant The Pump Room. As one measure of Melman's financial success, consider that he recently sold just two of his concepts to Brinker, International for close to $75 million.

But more impressive than his financial accomplishments have been Melman's W.O.W. relationships with the men and women who actually manage the day-to-day operations of his restaurants. LEYE, in fact, is nothing more than a collection of partners with a single commitment to excellence and innovation. Rather than build a top-down, vertical organization, Melman has proven that a horizontal model of equals can produce an incredibly profitable network of businesses which succeed on their own terms.

Marketing

Uncle Julio's: Creating a Legendary Family

When three alumni of the extraordinarily successful Pappas family of restaurants decided to strike out on their own, they knew that the restaurant business was more competitive than ever. If they expected to succeed, they would have to build a W.O.W. concept from the ground up, capable of evolving seamlessly with its customers' tastes. They wanted more than a theme—they were looking for a dynamic W.O.W. tool that would guide their entire company's marketing and customer experiences.

What they found, on a vacation to Mexico, was an old family album that eventually became the starting point of Uncle Julio's business journey. The restaurants now feature paintings and table photos featuring Uncle Julio's legendary kin: part fiction, part fact. As the company's journey has proven incredibly successful—they boast some of the highest individual restaurant volumes in the country—the journey of Uncle Julio's family has progressed too. Thanks to a legendary family tree, Uncle Julio's is one concept which shows no signs of becoming dated.

Change

Caribou Coffee, La Madeleine

Caribou Coffee founders John and Kim Puckett understand that the cookie cutter concept is a thing of the past. When they built their first Caribou Coffee units in Minneapolis several years ago, they were careful to make each one so different that customers would identify each neighborhood location on its own, not as part of a chain. Of course, this strategy defies the conventional wisdom that "concept" is more important than "comfort". It also disproves the conventional wisdom that successful concepts should be cloned from market to market. The result so far? Extraordinarily loyal customers at over 100 neighborhood stores. Moreover, Caribou need not worry that what works in Minneapolis will not work in Milwaukee, because they are constantly changing the concept to fit their unique environments.

La Madeleine, a fast-growing chain of 43 "French Bakery-Cafes", is another example of a company basing its success on a neighborhood-by-neighborhood vision. Founder Patrick Esquerre, a former advertising executive, came to America determined to provide authentic French breads and pastries close to twenty years ago. What began as a single French bakery in Dallas grew by word-of-mouth to become a phenomenon, and Esquerre has proven to be one of the few leaders capable of translating his initial success into promising growth. Each La Madeleine now features a cafe much larger than the bakery, and the unique quick-service restaurants achieve sales close to $2 million apiece. That's quite a bit more than McDonald's, without benefit of the hamburger chain's drive-through windows or playgrounds.

PART VI

The New Marketing Challenge:
Find the W.O.W. Niche

Customers 2000: The "More for Less" Generation

The new generation of Americans is the first whose standard of living will be lower than that of their parents. Economists predicted this trend many years ago, assuming a great deal of pessimism and anger to emerge from the so-called Gen Xers. Some even anticipated a "generational war", as nearly broke twenty-somethings fought for the retirement savings of their elders.

But that has not happened, and it probably won't. Why not?

The next generation has simply refused to accept a decline in their standard of living. In fact, they're experiencing a much higher standard of living than did their parents at a similar age—driving fancier cars, eating out more often, and buying expensive toys, like stereos and cellular phones. How is this possible without a corresponding increase in disposable income? They're saving little or nothing, and using credit. Last year, in fact, the total amount of consumer installment credit passed the $1 trillion mark, averaging over $12,000 per household. While their parents largely saved first and spent later, their children are spending now and expecting to pay later.

As you might guess, members of this generation have become extremely skilled consumers. Their imperative is simple: get more for less.

Take the restaurant industry as one example of how these consumers are demanding more value than ever. Prices at fast-food establishments have been pushed below the $1 mark at virtually all of the chains. Drive by a McDonald's, Wendy's or a Taco Bell and you'll see prices plastered on the windows. While analysts keep predicting that these prices "have to come up", they've largely stayed put. Recently, McDonald's unleashed a plan to push them down further. The direction is clear.

Casual dining establishments have also lowered prices to attract the next generation of consumers. Price has become one of the most important components of the product they serve. Whether steak and lobster or a bean burrito, customers demand to know "how much?" before coming in the door.

The "more for less" generation represents a dramatic shift in marketing focus. Whereas, in the past, restaurants found success by creating a special niche, they must now provide exceptional value, whatever the niche. That is a major reason why steakhouses like Old San Francisco and Outback, which provide the traditional "steakhouse" experience at a fraction of the traditional cost, have done so well in the 1990s. Customers want to be WOWed by value; we have to deliver more than we ever have for less than we ever have.

Advertising No Longer Works

In 1988, PepsiCo launched one of the most memorable advertising campaigns in history, featuring blues legend Ray Charles and a trio of beautiful vocalists singing a catchy tune: "You've got the right one baby, uh-Huh!" It just happened to be a failure. Despite the fact that nearly everyone heard—and remembered—the tune, which was promptly featured on cans, bottles and packages, the ads themselves didn't sell Pepsi. In fact, during the period of this promotion, Pepsi actually lost market share to its archrival Coca-Cola.

Last year, McDonald's experienced a similar advertising non-event. A $200 million advertising budget dedicated to the chain's new "Arch Deluxe" sandwich created a national sensation; the burger became a celebrity overnight, landing a full-color spot on the front page of *USA Today* and provoking opinion columns in countless newspapers and magazines. C.E.O. Mike Quinlan could barely contain his joy, calling it "by far the most successful product launch ever."

But, at the end of the day, quarterly sales at McDonald's stores fell 2%, while sales at Burger King, which had remained silent as its larger competitor basked in the media glow, rose 11%. Burger King chairman Robert Lowe joked that he'd sent Quinlan a thank-you note for introducing the Arch Deluxe, but had not received a reply.

What's happening?

Advertising, as we traditionally understand it, no longer works. While mass media events, like Pepsi's "uh-Huh" campaign and McDonald's Arch

Deluxe roll-out are still very successful at generating awareness, they have proven far less successful in generating sales. That's why so many companies are moving towards "high touch" marketing tools such as promotions and direct marketing, tools which require a purchase or produce a measurable response.

Lonnie Schiller, president of Express Foods in Houston, relates the story of an advertising agency which recently pitched his company, the owner of such concepts as Cafe Annie, Rio Ranch Steakhouse and Cafe Express. "They created great ads," he remarks, "very slick and clever. But at the end of the presentation, I realized that what these guys had created was no different from every other ad out there, and I couldn't figure out why anyone would notice them in particular." In other words, we've deluged our customers with so much advertising that it no longer touches them.

Marketing 2000 Is Knowledge

Marketing used to be the domain of the creative—the image builders. Now it is the territory of those who can accumulate the most knowledge. The most important component of successful advertising is no longer a clever tagline or a stunning visual, but a knowledge of where we can find customers who already want what we have to offer. As Stanley Marcus likes to say, we are moving from the paradigm of "broadcasting" to that of "narrowcasting." And the fuel of narrowcasting is knowledge.

Broadcasting is becoming outdated for two major reasons: inefficiency and cost. Consider the economics of a typical television ad or direct mail piece today. The television ad may reach 100,000 people, of whom maybe 100 or so will actually respond. The other 99,900 switched channels, got up to get something to eat, or simply ignored the ad. If you spent $1,000 on the ad, each response cost $10.

The direct mail piece probably fared slightly better—a 1% response is the norm—but mailing to these people also cost you far more: including printing, postage and mailing lists, you probably paid 25-30 cents per potential customer. In other words, if you mailed to those 100,000 television viewers, your cost was $25-$30 for every one person who responded. So, unless your product is expensive and very profitable, you almost certainly lost money by marketing.

We can no longer afford to spend our advertising budgets so unwisely. 1% redemption rates and even more abysmal returns from mass media simply can't justify what they remove from the bottom line. The challenge is not to be more clever, or more humorous, or cuter. The challenge is to find out who is already predisposed to buying our product, and touching them.

There are many tools to gather knowledge about customers, from simply talking to customers every day, as restaurant legend Norman Brinker is still fond of doing, to buying specialized mailing lists from companies with similar customers and cross-tabulating the data—essentially creating a profile of who your best customer is from a variety of sources. What is certain is that the more we listen to our existing customers, the more knowledge we possess to touch them in a way that will generate a reaction.

Our only consistent direct mail piece, for example, generates a response of over 50%—that's 50 times the industry average! We achieve this phenomenal response for two reasons: 1) the mailer goes out to customers who have dined with us before, and who we know enjoy our restaurants, and 2) the mailer wishes the customer a "happy birthday", and offers them a steak, on us. In other words, our knowledge of these customers allows us to create an extremely effective "high-touch" marketing tool.

Of course, there will always be the clever advertisements which spark a huge response, such as Wendy's Clara Peller asking "Where's the beef?" But such masterpieces of creative genius are very few and far between. Basing your company's success on your advertising agency's ability to W.O.W. an unknown group of potential customers is a losing battle. Learning about your customers and WOWing them yourself is a far more effective strategy.

Create a "High Touch" Message

Several years ago, a thirty-something entrepreneur by the name of Jim Koch took to the radio waves. His brewery, The Boston Beer Company, produced a microbrew called "Samuel Adams Lager". His message was simple: Samuel Adams was the best beer in America, bar none.

Samuel Adams's ads, which consisted of Koch talking about why his product was the best in what can only be described as an impassioned monotone, were anything but clever. Nor were they particularly funny or entertaining. Considering the advertising budgets against which his relatively tiny company was competing—the likes of Philip Morris (Miller) and Anheuser Busch (Budweiser)—many analysts wrote the Boston Beer Company's radio campaign off as a wasted effort. Koch was spending a few hundred thousand dollars to the beer giants' hundreds of millions.

Yet Koch's monologues became an overnight sensation in the beer world, where clarity of message and sincerity of tone were innovative ideas, and very "high touch". Pretty soon, the big guys stopped ignoring Koch and launched all-out assaults on everything from the quality of his product to the authenticity of his awards. Although, in the past year, Koch's company has suffered from the retribution of his giant competitors, the Boston Beer Company has proven an undeniable phenomenon, spawning dozens of imitators.

Koch's success with his modest radio budget illustrates a new reality very well: as advertising becomes more ubiquitous and in-your-face, content is becoming far more important than medium.

That is a monumental change. Back in the 1950s, it was probably enough just to be on the radio or television to make an impact. Today, customers are deluged with ads from McDonald's to the smallest mom- and pop-deli down the street. They've learned to listen to what really matters, and to sift through the special effects and clever copy.

Advertisers used to stake their claim on the amount of awareness they could generate, a process which depended heavily on mass media and big budgets. They predicted that anyone without access to the right media would fail, overshadowed by the advertising giants. But marketers like Koch prove that this assumption is flawed. Those who have something truly compelling to say will generally have a much higher impact at a lower volume than those with nothing new to communicate, no matter how loudly they decide to broadcast their message.

Find the W.O.W. Niche

We're talking about creating culture, not just celebrating culture.

Isaac Tigrett, founder, Hard Rock Cafe & House of Blues

Our marketing challenge today is to find the W.O.W. Niche. The old thinking defined niche in terms of specialization, bringing us dubious concepts like "quick-comfort home meal replacement". Our "2000" mentality defines the niche in terms of W.O.W. customer performance: how much excitement and entertainment can we generate? Consider the following examples of companies which have found the W.O.W. Niche and achieved extraordinary success:

Company Name	Average Unit Volume	WOW Niche
Hard Rock Cafe	$8-9 million	Rock 'N Roll Memorabilia
Cheesecake Factory	$9.2 million	Huge portions served in dramatic, upscale settings.
House of Blues	$9 million-plus	Live blues music.
Eatzi's	$10 million	Prepared foods and opera.
Planet Hollywood	$11 million	Movie Memorabilia
Rainforest Cafe	$14 million	Kid-friendly rainforest environment, complete with volcanoes and talking trees.

Each of these concepts has created a unique excitement and energy that WOWs customers. They have done so by ignoring the conventional wisdom that confines casual dining restaurants to 5,000 square-foot boxes with little differentiation in environment or menu, and they have achieved enviable success.

You may not expect your establishment to gross $8 million or more, but you should expect it to make customers respond in a positive way. You should make the experience different, interesting and energizing. Whether you're providing exceptional value, a stunning environment, innovative foods, impeccable service, or all of the above, you need to find the W.O.W. Niche. Otherwise, there is no guarantee that, among all of the cookie cutter concepts today, customers will find you.

Be The Best When You Get There

What's the rush? When you get there, just be the best.

Harris Pappas, Pappas Restaurants

Pappas restaurants are legendary creations. They can take years to build, but once open, they dominate the dining landscape wherever they are. Harris Pappas, one of the brothers behind the success, has grown his family's company from a little-known equipment supplier to a legendary chain achieving an estimated $400 million in annual sales. How? By living a simple maxim: that every restaurant experience—whether planned five minutes or five months in advance—is a destination.

Pappas, as his string of successful concepts testifies, knows how to be the best. To find the W.O.W. Niche, we must also realize that success is a function of creating incredible destinations, not mediocre "units"—we must practice W.O.W. and unlearn "Hurry up and fail."

Marketing Summary & Quick Check-up

Traditional

- Broadcasting
- Create Brand Awareness
- The Baby Boomer Generation
- Find A Narrowly Defined "Niche"
- Hurry Up and Fail
- Create a Message With Universal Appeal

W.O.W. 2000

- Narrowcasting
- Gain Customer Knowledge
- The "More For Less" Generation
- Create A Niche By WOWing Customers
- Be The Best When You Get There
- Create a "High Touch" Message Specific To Your Communities & Neighborhoods

Where You are Today

- Current Message/Tagline:

_____

_____

- Current Niche (Defined as a concept, e.g. products, service, prices, etc.):

_____

- Current Media Used: (Probably Print, Radio, T.V., etc .)

_____

- Current Customer Knowledge: (As a Group):

_____

_____

_____

Where You Want To Be Tomorrow

- W.O.W. Message (High-Touch)

_____

_____

- W.O.W. Niche (Defined as what makes your concept particularly exciting):

_____

- W.O.W. Media (e.g., Community Involvement, High-Touch Promotions):

_____

- W.O.W. Customer Knowledge (Individual Wants and Needs):

_____

_____

PART VII

What They Don't Teach You at Hamburger University:
Street Smarts

Ignore your 15 minutes of fame

Experienced entrepreneurs in the Boston area call it the "Kiss of Death". What they're referring to is the *Boston Globe*'s weekly profile of "up and coming" local businesses. The *Globe*, incidentally, is the most respected newspaper in the city, and its business writers do a fine job. The trouble is, the subjects of their adulation—young entrepreneurs—usually take the articles far too seriously; they simply don't understand the ephemeral nature of publicity.

Press coverage, especially the kind which declares your new concept an instant success, can be more dangerous than useful. It gives you a false sense of accomplishment, invests you in your young ways (even if they are flawed), and, often, exposes your best potential customers to your business when you are least prepared to impress them with the best product or service. Anyone can think of a restaurant which opened down the street to a good review and became the "hot spot", only to close within a few months. The problem? It became too crowded too quickly, and the food and service suffered. (As Yogi Berra once remarked, "Nobody goes there anymore—it's too crowded.")

Even worse than over-confidence, of course, is snobbery. Several years ago, a good friend and restaurant critic visited the hot new Italian restaurant with some guests from out of town. They had arrived early in the evening, and the dining room was nearly empty; so when the maitre d' sat them next to the kitchen, they felt slighted. My friend requested a table closer to the front, only for the maitre d' to reply "Those tables are reserved for our important guests." That restaurant has since declared bankruptcy.

Crystal Pepsi, the McLean Deluxe, and People Express all had their 15 minutes of fame. At the end of the day, the mountains of publicity simply accelerated their demise. If you open a new business, chances are good that you'll get your 15 minutes of fame. Ignore it.

Avoid Unnecessary Roadblocks

Last year, the federal government shut down for two weeks. Millions of people—federal workers, government contractors, retailers and overseas travelers, to name a few—were left holding the bag. By the time the shutdown was over, federal employees were demoralized, billions of dollars had been lost in the private sector, and millions of citizens were angry as hell.

What caused this monumental event? Apparently, our Speaker of the House was irked that our President had not paid him enough attention on Air Force One while traveling back from a trip to the Middle East. Is it any wonder why we think of the federal government as impossibly inefficient and gridlocked?

While admittedly less dramatic, we create unnecessary roadblocks in our businesses every day—roadblocks which cost us time, money and which demoralize and frustrate our business partners. How? We say something which someone else finds offensive; we react in a potentially effective, but insensitive manner; we ignore the merits of diplomacy to satisfy our personal expediency.

The solution is what we refer to at Old San Francisco as KWK: Killing With Kindness. Let me give you an example.

As I mentioned before, our restaurants achieve some of the highest volumes in the industry. The bad news is that many customers simply cannot get a table on busy nights unless they make their reservations well in advance. We constantly remind them to make reservations early, but every week, we receive a phone call from someone insisting that they be seated at our busiest time the following Saturday night. We explain that there are only so many tables and generally offer an earlier time, say 5:30 rather than 6:30.

Our hostess knows that this person will show up with his party at 6:00 or 6:15, not 5:30. And when they do, she has a choice: she can give them the evil eye and tell them that another party has their table at 8:00 p.m., creating all sorts of acrimony, or she can greet them with an even wider smile than usual, and show them to their table without any mention of time. She does the latter.

Why? Because the customer has already won—he's received the table when he really wanted it. Moreover, the customer *should* have won, and we should be happy to accommodate him and his guests. If we tried to bend their experience to our scheduling once they arrived, we would only make the experience take longer (because their reaction would be to defend their right to linger as long as they wanted to) and make things very unpleasant, indeed. We choose to focus our efforts on making any additional waits imposed on other customers as enjoyable as possible, efforts which I will discuss in a later chapter.

Think about all of the unnecessary misunderstandings you have had in the past several months with employees and customers alike; then think of the ultimate resolution. Was it worth the extra five or ten minutes (or longer) of extended conflict when the end result was exactly the same as it would have been had you not become angry or antagonistic? Probably not. So kill them with kindness.

Don't Achieve Too Much Success

Diplomats often make the egregious error of failing to realize the

consequences of achieving too much success.

Henry Kissinger

Remember the old saying "If it's too good to be true, it probably is"?
Let me give you one example. In the past couple of years, good retail locations have become very hard to find; in fact, finding real estate is probably an even more competitive business than finding customers! Landlords have benefited hugely from this seller's market, as an increasing number of retailers fight for relatively few prime locations. The laws of supply and demand have swung almost completely to their favor.

The trouble is, a landlord's ability to negotiate a sweet deal for himself can easily create an unprofitable deal for the tenant. In the beginning, the tenant may be willing to pay a steep price in order to gain a desired location, but, if the deal is too much in the landlord's favor, the tenant will sustain losses and eventually stop paying its rent. A number of restaurant chains—Sizzler and Sfuzzi are two examples—have even declared bankruptcy as a means to escape or renegotiate their lease obligations at unprofitable locations. In this case, their landlords—the ones who thought they had negotiated such a terrific deal for themselves—cannot collect rent *or* find new tenants until the bankruptcy court judge approves (a process which can literally take months). Had they simply negotiated a deal which made sense for their tenants as well as for themselves, they would probably be better off.

Franchisors, who hold powers similar to landlords, can also negotiate too successfully with their franchisees. The larger the franchise system becomes, for example, the more control franchisors typically build into their franchise agreements. Feeling powerless to change much of anything in the contracts, franchisees generally play along, agreeing to restrictive terms and conditions which can literally make it impossible for them to succeed. In the end, the obvious happens: I know of several restaurant chains which have re-purchased stores from franchisees simply to avoid lawsuits, a lose/lose scenario for both parties.

Whenever you negotiate with vendors, landlords, franchisees, or even customers, both sides of the equation should make sense, not just the terrific deal that you can arrange for yourself. Remember that you will be living with their success or failure as well as your own.

Avoid Being Prematurely Right

Managers often make the unavoidable, but altogether fatal,

mistake of being prematurely right.

Peter F. Drucker

I don't know how many times people have told me that Americans will stop eating red meat. They may be right, but their timing is definitely wrong. Steakhouses, including ours, are thriving as never before. Beef consumption actually went up a little last year, not down. Meanwhile, I know of several vegetarian restaurants and juice bars that shuttered their doors last year, even as sales at steakhouses skyrocketed.

In business, it's simply not enough to be right. *You must be right at the right time.* Otherwise, what you think is not only wrong, but irrelevant.

Don't Let Perception = Reality

We began to run into trouble when we started

to believe we were really the Beatles.

George Harrison

Too many businesses are run from the outside in, rather than from the inside out. In other words, too many organizations begin with a perception of success which they try to turn into a reality, rather than with a successful reality which will automatically reap positive perceptions.

Trying to change perceptions rather than actualities is a tempting strategy—it appears to be so much easier to change perception than reality—but the end result is failure in both areas.

Consider, for example, how many billions of dollars food advertisers spend each year trying to create the perception of a perfect hamburger. They hire food "stylists" to position the product in the best possible light, then project it up on billboards surrounded by gardens of fresh vegetables or scores of smiling faces. When the customer actually visits the store, however, they're faced with the same squashed burger inside waxed paper. The net result? Customers have become extremely distrustful of both advertisements and advertisers in general. In fact, a recent Gallup Poll found that just under 80% of teenagers believe that advertising does not represent products truthfully.

No perception is ever more important than the reality you deliver in your establishment. McDonald's Quarter Pounder is a perfect example. When the sandwich first came out, the Company was flooded with complaints from disappointed customers. Why? The burger wasn't anything near a quarter pound of meat. Since then, all advertisers have been forced to add the small print "weight before cooking" in their ads.

At Old San Francisco, our ad budget is relatively small, our message is more descriptive than sensational, and any advertisements you see of ours show the food exactly how it is presented in our restaurants. Does this make us less appealing to potential customers? Not at all. We have the best customers in the business, and some of the most famous.

A couple of years ago, for example, Mick Jagger and his entourage decided to drop in to our San Antonio restaurant for dinner. Last year, we fed Elton John and his touring band in Houston. We are a regular choice for sports celebrities like Deion Sanders and David Robinson. Actually, despite the fact that we advertise far less than any of our competitors, many of whom are national chains, we probably have established a more powerful name for ourselves than virtually anyone. How? By focusing on who we are, not who we think the general public would like us to be.

Don't Say What You Can Do

Just Do It

Nike Slogan

At Old San Francisco, we have a simple rule: *if you can do it, do it, don't say it*. This rule not only prevents us from wasting huge amounts of time talking about what we *might* (or might not) do tomorrow, it prevents us from creating expectations over and above what we can accomplish today, or committing ourselves too far into the future.

A lot of managers love to talk about their goals years from now. A lot of them also like to make bold predictions, because they think that boldness shows commitment. At least, that's the theory. But what tends to happen in reality is that either the plans don't materialize—and the manager's credibility is weakened—or the plans do materialize, but in a far more rigid manner than they should have. In other words, talking about what you're going to do rather than simply doing it not only risks failure, but inflexibility.

We focus our efforts—and those of our employees—on the present, a philosophy which we all know by "TNT" (Today, Not Tomorrow), for a very simple reason: if we don't take care of our business today, there won't be a tomorrow. If we do a superb job and W.O.W. our customers today, our tomorrows will be many and profitable. There is simply no substitute for immediate action.

Don't Be Too Afraid Of The Dark

Instant gratification takes too long.

Carrie Fisher, Postcards From The Edge

Business decisions are rarely made in broad daylight, with absolute clarity of knowledge. So if you're not comfortable operating in the dark sometimes—if you need instant gratification from each decision—you'll fail.

I've seen plenty of managers whose intentions were noble, but whose fear of the dark eventually got the better of them. Instead of staying the course, they decided to reverse direction midway, and retreat to known ground; they forgot the simple fact that once you're halfway to your destination, it's just as easy to keep moving forward as it is to go back. Not that you shouldn't express doubts and remember that your judgment is fallible—but you should also deal with your fears before you walk the next step. If you deal with fear first, you won't question yourself at precisely the moments when you have the most opportunity to succeed: when everyone else is paralyzed by similar fears.

Not long ago, a group of teenagers on a high-school trip got caught in a blizzard on Mount Hood, which is located in the Pacific Northwest. Tragically, out of more than a dozen original campers, only two survived. Days after the two survivors had walked back to the bottom of the mountain, their friends were found where they had stopped, frozen in a single pile. When asked why he had been able to continue on while most of his friends gave in to fatigue, one of the survivors remarked that he knew if he kept walking in the same direction, he would eventually get out of the storm.

We may not always be comfortable that we know the right direction, but, eventually, our consistent efforts will take us to a better place.

So What? Next.

Everybody poops.

Ben Cohen, founder, Ben & Jerry's

I'm not sure why so many of us find it so hard to face up to criticism, to admit that we don't have the answer or that we screwed up.

Perhaps that is why it is refreshing to listen to a leader like Bill Marriott. Marriott, best known for the hotels which bear his name, redefined the standards of customer service around the world. He has built both the largest hotel chain in the world and one of the country's largest foodservice companies. He is not someone you would expect to talk about failure.

But that's exactly what he did when a talk-show host recently asked "have you ever made a bad decision?" Marriott, without missing a beat, replied "Well, we had a beautiful hotel in Panama (reduced to rubble by war)," and went on to list a number of other failed ventures, laughing and smiling all the while. Marriott was clearly not only unabashed about his failures, but decidedly proud of them. They were, he explained, the price of the Company's successes elsewhere.

Because we encourage our own employees to take so many risks—to step outside of the boundaries and W.O.W. their customers—we experience our share of failures at Old San Francisco. We also experience *more* than our fair share of programs which just do not work—everything from the sports celebrity who doesn't live up to his promotional commitments to the promising new menu item that simply doesn't sell. A few years ago, we had to stop our practice of allowing adults on our bar swing because one of our overenthusiastic (and overly inebriated) patrons literally kicked one of our servers off of the bar. All of these disappointments make us think and change; what they don't do is convince us to stop and give up.

A few years ago, our employees borrowed the phrase "Some Will; Some Won't; So What? Next" from a friend named Jim Chism. It's a constant reminder of the inevitability of failures, and the absolute necessity of resilience.

PART VIII

The New Vision:
Forget What You Think You Know

How Conventional Wisdom Misleads You

A decade ago, all of the "experts" were predicting a dramatic shift to healthier lifestyles. This meant that most Americans would choose to exercise rather than watch television, lose weight rather than gain it, and eat healthier meals like skinless chicken and frozen yogurt rather than thick steaks and cheesecake. These self-proclaimed lifestyle gurus were unanimous, and the media published their predictions as fact. The conventional wisdom said that Americans would be leading vastly healthier lifestyles today.

Yet every statistic shows that we actually exercise less, watch more television (although some of this time is now being spent on the Internet), and weigh more than we did ten years ago. Furthermore, most of the frozen yogurt stores which sprung up almost overnight to satiate America's new obsession with health have shut down, and most of those that remain now serve high-fat ice cream and cookies. Meanwhile, steakhouse chains like Outback and Lonestar experienced astronomical growth, and super-premium ice creams and decadent desserts have become some of the most popular food items on menus across the country.

What happened?

Conventional wisdom was, in many ways, right on target. But it was also fundamentally incorrect, thanks to huge flaws in context and misleading assumptions. Here's a list of the three ways in which conventional wisdom consistently misleads:

1) Assume that people will do what they say they will.

Ten years ago, people may very well have been interested in leading healthier lifestyles. They were certainly very happy to say so to whoever was listening—it made them feel more fashionable and less guilty. But the majority exercised their right to say one thing and do another.

2) Overstate the degree of change

While the "experts" predicted massive changes which would revolutionize lifestyles, most Americans were thinking far more modestly— switch to 2% milk from whole, for example, or go walking for 2 miles a few times a week. They never planned on becoming American Gladiators.

3) Assume that people will always act in their own best interests

Ever since Adam Smith published *The Wealth of Nations* in 1776, we have been taught that people will do what is in their self-interest. But environment and marketing both affect people's perceptions of self-interest. When steakhouses, for example, started offering better value, people were compelled to take advantage. New cable channels and satellite dishes brought people programming which trumped their desire to be healthier.

And so on.

The experts are once again beating the drums of the "healthy lifestyle revolution", though more cautiously than before. They point to data showing that more people are choosing vegetarian alternatives, and that super-premium ice cream sales have leveled off. Their data may be true, but, as we know from past experience, it does not necessarily mean that the revolution is imminent.

Forget What You Think You Know

Most of our assumptions begin as honest assessments based on previous experiences. The trouble is, the longer we hold on to them, the more likely it is that these assumptions have become outdated, or, simply wrong. Remember how American car-makers assumed that no one would ever buy a Japanese car that cost more than $20,000? Then came the Acura, the Infinity and the Lexus. Today, I don't hear American manufacturers declaring price ceilings on Japanese cars. They've learned their lesson.

Still, it's amazing how tenacious we can be of beliefs which are obviously mistaken. I've seen countless restaurant managers swear that a certain employee couldn't possibly be stealing from them, even as their costs skyrocketed and sales at the times when this employee was working the cash register mysteriously dropped. Their logic is always the same: "He would never steal from me. I know this person." My response is "You *think* you know this person. But what you think you know is wrong." You have to remove the blinders caused by what you want to believe in order to confront the realities of your situation. And the more comfortable you become with your own assumptions, the more difficult it is to face the realities.

The principle of forgetting what you think you know explains why some of the restaurant industry's most successful companies have been led by outsiders—people who knew little or nothing about restaurants, and therefore, people who had little or nothing to "unlearn." One such example is Spaghetti Warehouse, a concept founded by a former Tandy Corp.

executive in Dallas, Texas. Defying virtually every observer, this executive built a huge restaurant in an abandoned warehouse situated in a virtually dead urban area. Its only selling points? Wonderful food, cheap prices, and a unique atmosphere, to say the least—Spaghetti Warehouse diners were led to tables within train cars, or seated at booths made from antique bedposts. The concept was an immediate hit, and Spaghetti Warehouse eventually expanded to more than 30 locations. Today, that formerly abandoned warehouse's neighbors include the pricey Palm restaurant, Planet Hollywood, an ice-skating rink, Landry's Seafood House, T.G.I. Friday's and many other large national chains. The original restaurant remains one of the company's top-performers. Ironically, however, it was Spaghetti Warehouse's ill-fated expansion into suburban restaurant rows—the places that experts told them were sure bets—that has stalled further growth plans, at least for now.

Those of us who are already in the industry, who have built careers and/or companies, must never forget what we don't know. We must be both "open" to opportunities which defy our old assumptions and "willing" to pursue them.

What You Think Doesn't Matter

Let your customers dress up and dress down your restaurant.

Tilman Fertitta, founder, Landry's Seafood Restaurants

Last year, a number of prominent New York establishments—including the legendary '21' Club and the Four Seasons Restaurant—finally nixed their tie requirements for male customers. Had they listened to Fertitta's advice, they might have abandoned the old policy much sooner. Instead, these establishments lost millions in business by insisting that all of their customers observe a formality largely out of touch with today's lifestyles.

Like these New York restaurants, many of us put too much weight behind what *we* think. But the more we value the thoughts of others—especially our customers—the more business we gain, and the better prepared we are for the future. Let me share two examples:

Last year, the largest chain of bagel bakeries in the country built their first store in Texas; they are based in Vermont. Thinking that what worked in the Northeast should work in Texas, the chain steadfastly refused to offer customers the option of having their bagel toasted. *They* knew better. This may not sound like a big deal, but in a state whose favorite bread is called "Texas Toast", the chain's no-toast rule angered more than a few customers. After enduring several months worth of complaints and lost sales, this chain will now gladly toast your bagel.

Also last year, an extremely successful Italian restaurant in Dallas opened its second unit, just ten miles away from the original. Because the original location had established a reputation as something of a "meet market"—a reputation which helped boost bar sales considerably—the second restaurant was in no mood to accommodate young children; after all, what would drive singles away faster than screaming babies? So the managers decided not to order high chairs.

What those managers thought was an easy solution turned out to be a total disaster. From day one, the restaurant's waitstaff were confronted with a stream of screaming parents—not babies!—angered that their young children had no place to sit but on their laps. Within three months, this place had plenty of high-chairs, and this year, its sales are up over 20%. Like the chain of bagel bakeries, the managers thought that what worked in one market would work in an entirely different area. They also believed that they knew better than their customers. They were wrong, and they quickly learned how to listen.

Restaurants are not alone in listening more and dictating less. Successful businesses everywhere are tuning in to their customers, and, as a result, dramatically changing the products and services they offer. Proctor & Gamble, for example, sells no less than twenty kinds of pampers today, up from one a few decades ago; Johnson & Johnson sells Tylenol a.m., Tylenol Cold, Tylenol Capsules and Tylenol p.m., not just Tylenol; The Olive Garden may be a national restaurant chain, but, with well over 100 different versions of its menu in existence, it is really more like a collection of many regional dining places.

Today's business environment is simply too diverse and fast-paced to ignore *any* customers. To paraphrase entertainment mogul David Geffen: "There's what you think and what your customers think. What you think doesn't matter."

What You Don't Know Kills You

When I was twenty-two years old, I knew everything. I had been a chef, kitchen manager, restaurant manager and maitre d', and I'd witnessed every mistake that had ever been made. There was absolutely no doubt in my mind that it was time to strike out on my own. So I opened a restaurant called "Barrister's"—named after my best customers, who also patronized the courthouse next door.

For a while, the restaurant did well, and my ego was gratified. But then, within a year of opening, something terrible happened: the courthouse moved several miles away! So here I was, with my "Barrister's" restaurant, and not a single lawyer in sight! Needless to say, our business dried up and I felt like a total failure. It took me seven years to pay off all of our suppliers (which I did, in full and with interest), and it cost me precious relationships with college friends and family members, some of whom are creditors to this day. I'm not sure that those relationships can ever be restored in full.

Had I simply talked to a few more people, I would have known of the courthouse's planned move, and I could have waited to build my restaurant. Or I could have built a totally different concept elsewhere. But I didn't. I went ahead and built an impending disaster because I was convinced that I knew it all.

The most successful people are those who know what they don't know. They worry about what's down the road, not about what they can already see. They ignore their present success and seek out the opinions of others. They sacrifice their ego and gain a wealth of knowledge. They are open to do whatever it takes to deliver great customer performance.

Like Barrister's, most businesses fail because of unforeseen circumstances; they get blindsided from a direction which they've chosen to ignore. I say chosen because I think that most of us have the choice to use our perceptions and intelligence. Wearing blinders is not forced upon any of us.

Let me give you a more recent example. Blockbuster Video, the extraordinarily successful chain of video stores, is in a bind. The reason? Video rentals are on their way down.

That's not surprising. After all, analysts have been predicting that satellite dishes and new, movies-on-demand technology would make video rentals obsolete. What is surprising is the *reason* that video rentals are down. It's not technology which is stealing Blockbuster's business, but what the industry calls "sell-through": videotape sales.

Why has sell-through become an issue? Because several years ago studios realized that they could make far more money by selling their movies to an unlimited number of consumers rather than to a limited number of video stores. Instead of selling 100,000 copies of "Aladdin" at $80 a pop to rental stores, for example, Disney will sell 20 million of those videos at retail for $19.95 and make 50 times as much money! Blockbuster's blinders prevented executives from seeing that the traditional method of distribution was not the most profitable for its suppliers—the studios; it is now facing entirely new competitors like Wal-Mart, K-Mart and even McDonald's without a coherent strategy.

Sustaining success usually proves tougher than achieving it. Learning what you don't know is the only way to stay ahead of your current competitors as well as prepare for the new ones you will face down the road.

The restaurant industry is cluttered with what I call "me-too"s: concepts that copy the formulas of proven winners rather than establish their own identities.

There is nothing wrong with playing follow the leader now and then. But to expect that success can be cloned is wishful thinking—today's business arena is simply too competitive. To make it work, you cannot *just* be a "me-too" concept; you must provide a *superior* alternative to what already exists—one that operates more efficiently, provides more value, is consistently more "high-touch" or produces noticeably better products.

That's where the "me-too"s usually fail. Instead of entering an older market segment where customers may be hungry for a superior alternative, "me-too"s almost always choose to enter relatively new, fast-growing markets. Why? Because the creators of "me-too" concepts think that the higher the rate of sales growth, the bigger the opportunity; hence the flood of bagel and juice bar concepts. What they fail to understand is what lies behind that growth: one or a few existing competitors doing an outstanding job of meeting customers' needs. *A well-managed concept fuels the demand for particular products, not vice-versa.*

Starbucks Coffee provides an excellent example of this point. The chain of coffee cafes, which is more than twenty-five years old, began attracting national attention in the early 1990s. Starbucks' fast growth created a sort of coffee "craze" that did not go unnoticed by hundreds, if not thousands, of aspiring entrepreneurs. When they saw Starbucks' success and the resulting growth of the coffee cafe market, they rushed in. After all, what could be so complicated about selling coffee?

But not only did the coffee business prove deceptively complex—and subject to severe price fluctuations—Starbucks proved a formidable competitor. Although it was rarely the first coffee cafe in any market, Starbucks was always the first to offer the Starbucks experience, which is where the real demand has proven to be. The concepts which have not provided a better or more unique experience have failed.

Sometimes, a little imitation can yield positive results. Papa John's, for example, has injected W.O.W. into a relatively unexciting segment of the industry—pizza—with a quality-focused message and some innovative marketing. But, for the most part, an aggressive, successful opponent is a warning sign to stay away. In other words, the "hot" segment you hoped to enter may turn out to be as cold as yesterday's latte.

"Nobody Else Does It" = Opportunity

Just out of college, I became a manager of a restaurant with a loyal, if modest, following. At the time, the restaurant only served dinner on the weekends. Had I polled most of the staff, I suspect that they either wouldn't have cared whether or not we tried to offer any other meals (as long as it didn't affect their schedules), or, they would have responded that since nobody else did it, going outside the dinner business probably wasn't a good idea.

Within the space of a few months, I started serving lunch. Then I opened up an entirely new section on the patio where we hosted cook-outs for the families who came to see their kids play soccer on the fields next door, as well as for the fans who came every week in season to see the professional teams. Sales, obviously, went through the roof—not only at these new times, but also at dinner, since we were creating so much more exposure for the restaurant. I did not stop to wonder why other restaurants didn't do these things; all I knew was that touching people before dinner was an opportunity for us to increase our own business.

I've never understood the rationale that if something was worth doing, someone else would already be doing it. Not only is it wrong, it's completely defeatist—much like the early 20th century thinkers who declared that everything had already been invented.

Actually, two of the highest-volume days in our restaurants today are Christmas and Thanksgiving. It's no coincidence that these are both days when most of our competitors are closed. The fact that they ignore the 5,000 customers whom we serve on both of these days has proven a hugely profitable opportunity for us. Why aren't they doing it? Their perceived boundaries—whether their own or a franchisor's—won't let them do whatever it takes to make it happen.

For restaurants today, there are plenty of opportunities to create new business such as catering, take-out, delivery, and even ready-to-heat meal preparation. If you're not involved in these businesses already, don't wait until all of your competitors are.

Re-positioning—changing the customer's perception of a product rather than the product itself—doesn't work. Changing the label and the advertising, but nothing else, constitutes a non-event that our customers quickly learn to ignore.

As a result, we have chosen to ignore re-positioning. We would never, for example, change the names of our restaurants from "Old San Francisco" to "New San Francisco". We've learned from experience—New Coke's experience, to be precise. In the mid-eighties, the Coca-Cola Co. was losing market share to archrival Pepsi. So Coke made some minor changes to its formula—it added some carbonation—and re-positioned its core product as "New Coke". The resulting fiasco is familiar to most of us, and it resulted in the return of the original Coke (Coca-Cola Classic) even though the vast majority of customers couldn't tell the difference between new and old. Observers are still mixed on whether or not the publicity Coke gained ended up benefiting the company, but what is clear is that New Coke totally bombed.

Considering that the vast majority of companies will never reap the kind of publicity afforded a mega-brand like Coke's re-positioning, the net result of re-positioning tends to run the gamut from irrelevant to harmful. Why? When a brand tries to re-position itself, it abandons its old cadre of loyal customers, betting that it will find a much larger market. But new customers rarely materialize so easily, and, more often than not, companies actually end up swinging back in the other direction: begging old customers to forgive them. That is how Coca-Cola brought back Coca-Cola Classic to its angry customers; the Company said, in essence: "We screwed up. Here's the product which we never should have changed in the first place."

Another good example of a re-positioning disaster is Jack-In-The-Box. Jack-In-The-Box—a national fast-food chain—spent decades building its name brand before a new advertising agency had the brilliant idea of blowing it all up, literally. Convincing the chain's executives that the Company's "Jack" mascot was too childlike, the agency produced a series of ads decimating the lovable Jack with dynamite. Now, some people had a real affection for Jack; others probably cared less, but no customers were banging down the Company's doors calling for the death of Jack; yet that, of course, is exactly what they did.

It took the Company many years of losses to realize its huge mistake. Where the Company had stood for something, it now had no vehicle to connect with its customer base. Furthermore, its "re-positioning" to more serious, adult customers just kept digging it into a deeper and deeper hole. The more they talked about how different they were, the more existing customers became alienated.

Last year, Jack returned, thanks to yet another advertising agency. And sales at Jack-In-The-Box suddenly started climbing again—actually they took off into the double digits, while most of the chain's competitors were witnessing declines. I can't recall how they explained Jack's resurrection (a potentially W.O.W. event, if there ever was one), but customers apparently didn't care about that either. They were just relieved to see a familiar face.

PART IX

The Modern Toolbox:
High-Tech and High-Touch

Technology Determines Your Speed

While we use the equation "E=MC^2" to show that effort determines *what* we accomplish, technology is beginning to play an important role by determining the *speed* with which we realize those accomplishments. Using the right technology turbocharges your efforts; ignoring useful technology can leave you far behind, languishing in the dust of your competitors.

There are several technologies which all hospitality businesses should use. Databases and the World Wide Web are explained in the next two chapters. Others include e-mail and sophisticated point-of sale technologies. E-mail encourages people to communicate quickly; it also allows for unfiltered—and, therefore, more accurate—communication between senior-level people and employees on the front line.

Point-of-sale technologies, on the other hand, have revolutionized the way we do business at the unit level. Today, our sales terminals can instantly tell us what's selling (and what's not). Managers can use the data to change the product mix, and even re-structure entire menus daily to meet real demand. We can react to our customers' changing tastes much faster today than we could in the past.

Despite the obvious benefits, new technology will always be a means to improve the customer performance supplied by our people, and not a replacement for it. As managers, our job is to create environments where high-tech and high-touch work together.

The database is the single most powerful new technology at our disposal. The database allows us to keep track of individual customers efficiently. If you aren't keeping track of your customers (either by capturing their data directly into your P.O.S. system or using a simple "guest book")—as well as some basic information like recent purchases and average spending—you're losing essential knowledge.

Less is More

Unfortunately, many of us treat our databases as a name accumulation game. But in my experience, the more names you accumulate, the *less* effective your database will actually be. Why? Because, generally speaking, the more names you enter in, the less likely you are to know much about them. And the less you know about your database customers, the less effective your marketing program.

Let me give you one example. Last year, a major casual dining chain initiated a frequent customer program. Same-store sales had been slipping for several quarters, and executives were eager to show Wall Street that they had a plan to bring customers back. The program they launched was aggressive. Customers who patronized the restaurants were handed an application with a frequent dining card after their meal. If they chose to fill out the application, they were immediately awarded the card, and given a certificate for a free dessert. The program itself would keep track of future purchases and send them awards as they accumulated points. These awards ranged from free food to airplane tickets.

The great news was that this company quickly accumulated over 3 million "frequent customers". The bad news was that their list was instantly too large to be manageable. The truly loyal customers who the company wished to reward were treated exactly the same as the one-time visitors who simply wanted the free dessert or felt pressured to fill out the application. In other words, the Company accumulated a database of people who liked to eat dessert for free, not a list of people who would be particularly loyal to their chain! Recently, the chain abandoned the program, citing high maintenance costs.

Potential User > Light User > Heavy User

The simple flowchart above represents the heart of any successful database strategy. You should encourage forward movement (increasing the number of times a customer uses your product), and have a plan to counter any backward movement (when customers begin to use less of your product). If your list becomes too full of one kind of person, e.g. potential users, or if you can't determine who's who, your database marketing program is going to be basically useless. If, however, you begin with a manageable number of records, and can easily determine what kinds of customers you've got, creating the right incentives becomes easy.

One of my favorite examples of a successful database marketing strategy is Pizza Hut Delivery, which has used an incredibly sophisticated system to track the buying patterns of its customers. Because the customers give their telephone number and address every time they buy a pizza, Pizza Hut's database can track their buying habits in real time. It can then produce customized incentives to turn light users into regular customers, as well as reminders for store managers to contact customers who have stopped eating pizza or who have switched to competitors.

A much different—but no less effective—example is the Mansion on Turtle Creek in Dallas, whose concierge staff keeps track of frequent guests' preferences on filed index cards. When a guest makes a reservation, their file is pulled, and the hotel staff is able to fulfill their individual desires the moment they walk in the door. For the past several years, the Mansion on Turtle Creek has been named the top luxury hotel in the world by *The Robb Report.*

The database need not be high-tech, but it must always be high-touch.

The World Wide Web - Interactivity

As we head into a new Millennium, the television's dominance of American entertainment is finally being seriously challenged by interactive media: personal computers, more sophisticated video games, and, of course, the Internet. Interactive tools are not gaining ground because they are better at entertaining than the television per se, but because they are capable of far more than the "boob tube". Customers can plan vacations, balance their checkbook, communicate with others, and do an increasing number of tasks easier with the interactive tools. More importantly, perhaps, is the fact that they can do many of these things cheaper than before. As you read this book, for example, thousands of Americans are using the Internet to get a less expensive airplane ticket for the holidays.

Restaurateurs have always been interactive by nature. The best, like Norman Brinker, have been the most interactive on a personal level, soliciting customer advice wherever and whenever possible. Restaurateurs have also realized the importance of price—providing a financial incentive to walk in the door. In order to succeed in the years ahead, we must use the new technologies both to achieve a higher level of interactivity, and to gain (or retain) customers by providing better financial incentives.

Information

What makes a marketing tool interactive? Any mechanism which allows for the two-way exchange of information. At the very least, an interactive medium should provide information on the company or product; a more sophisticated marketer will add an incentive to buy. In return, companies should find out who their customers are and where opportunities exist to serve them better. Of course, old technologies like direct mail and customer comment cards accomplish this degree of interactivity, but they do it very slowly. Technologies like computerized frequent buyer programs or Websites make the exchange of information faster and more fun.

The World Wide Web

The World Wide Web is the flagship technology of interactivity. In fact, no medium has ever been so efficient at soliciting customer feedback, or molding a targeted response to it instantaneously. The trouble is that there is not much reliable information on the Web itself. Current estimates of the number of Web sites, for example, range from 170,000 to 2 million, a huge divergence.

Another problem is that the wider the Web's audience becomes, the less targeted a vehicle it is. For example, if your company sets up a Web site, you must decide whether to target customers, franchisees, licensees, vendors or all of the above. You need to keep in mind, of course, that journalists, competitors and salesmen will be looking at your page as well as your target groups. In fact, any ideas which you incorporate into your Web page may magically appear in the press or on other Web pages the following day! Perhaps even sooner! So the Web is a phenomenal tool for soliciting input and reaching out to customers, but it's still misunderstood.

At the end of the day, what matters is that the interaction between customer and company is positive; yet technology does precious little to provide good food, warm service, or a clean restaurant. So, unfortunately, new advertising technologies will probably make the same mistakes as the old—hyping the concept rather than accumulating information to deliver a consistently excellent experience.

I hope that you'll visit Old San Francisco on the Web (and even make a reservation, if you're in town). Our URL (Web address) is: osfsteakhouse.com.

PART X

The New Leadership Challenge: *Change*

Redefine Leadership

The essence of leadership today is to make

sure that the organization knows itself.

Mort Meyerson, Perot Systems

Most people know that Ted Turner founded CNN. What they don't realize is that he had little hands-on contact with the channel in its early days. While a few young executives were putting CNN on the air, Turner was in Australia winning the America's Cup.

Turner, like many entrepreneurs, is simply not a manager. He is an "idea man": a brilliant mind with an unusual understanding of what people want. The fact that he has become a multi-billionaire has less to do with his ability to manage than his ability to conceptualize successful concepts. In fact, had Turner tried to lead the CNN project, it probably wouldn't have survived his infamous changes of focus. There would have been no one to stay the course.

Where Turner did do a brilliant job was fostering his vision, and making sure that the path was clear for his chosen leaders to succeed. Turner's leadership was a function of foresight, not a version of "command-and-control." Similarly, I like to think of our job as hospitality managers in terms of removing the obstacles that stand in the way of our employees so that they can deliver great customer performance. We must clarify and protect our vision across the organizations we manage rather than simply bark orders.

I'm not sure why the hospitality industry continues to operate in such a hierarchical manner, with general managers and assistant managers on top, and employees (and ultimately customers) on the bottom. Most of us are mired in systems that were set up long we were even born; we can learn a lot about leadership from high-tech entrepreneurs like Meyerson and Turner.

Rich Melman, a terrific leader and founder of Lettuce Entertain You Enterprises, is one of the few exceptions to the top-down management paradigm. He likes to remind his managers that his job is enabling their success. If he were only interested in doing the best job himself, he quips, he'd own a hot dog stand, not the $150 million restaurant conglomerate he heads today.

Nordstrom, Inc., operator of the upscale department stores, revolutionized leadership in its business by creating the "upside down" management chart. Instead of the CEO at the top and employees at the base, their "inverted pyramid" shows customers at the top, then employees, and finally, at the very bottom, executives. Redefining leadership can begin with the simple act of posting your current organizational chart upside down—just make sure that your managers and executives are capable of supporting your people at the top, or the entire organization will stumble.

Create a Mission of Values, Not Destinations

- We serve our customers with innovative, responsive solutions to their needs.

- We treasure our people by attracting, developing, and recognizing outstanding people, and caring for them and their families.

- We operate with integrity by treating our customers, people, and suppliers in a fair and honest manner—as we want to be treated.

- We reward our stakeholders by producing strong financial performance from which everyone benefits.

- We contribute to our community by using our talents and resources to better the conditions in the diverse communities in which we work.

Perot Systems Corporation Value Statement

The five statements on the previous page are printed on small cards and carried by every employee of Perot Systems. They represent the values upon which the company is based; collectively, they form the company's mission statement. These statements have proven to be extremely successful—in fact, Perot Systems has grown even faster than Electronic Data Systems, the first company which made the founder of both companies, Ross Perot, a multi-billionaire.

Not that adding to its namesake's fortune is the goal of Perot Systems; it is not. A majority of the company is owned by its employees. The goal of Perot Systems is to not only enjoy success, but to create it in a manner which benefits everyone.

Imagine how different the company would be if its mission were to reach $1 billion in sales within five years; or to go public within six years, making all of its executives millionaires. These second types of goals— based on destinations and not values—are the ones which so many of us aspire to; if we don't make them part of our explicit mission statement, we certainly internalize them as personal goals. We don't care so much about the journey as the destination.

A few simple truths that deserve repeating: it is *within* the journey to become successful that we will spend the vast majority of our time. It is *within* the journey that we will be forced to be flexible, and perhaps change our assumptions. It is *within* the journey that we will establish our identity, our reputations, and the W.O.W. relationships which will bring us happiness and success in the future. The destination, if, indeed, we ever find one, is ephemeral.

I can't count the number of businesspeople who try to impress others by bragging about where they're headed—the number of restaurants they'll open next year is a favorite—even when they have no idea *how* they're going to get there. Not surprisingly, their dreams rarely materialize. Somewhere down the road, their goals literally fall apart. Why? They have no direction, only financial milestones to serve their leaders.

Invariably, the companies which experience the most success are those which make their financial goals by-products of their values, and not vice-versa. Their directions never change; as a result, their consistent effort takes them to extraordinary destinations.

Seek first to understand, and then to be understood.

Steven Covey

Listening in order to change—often called "empathetic listening"—is ultimately the only kind of listening that matters.

When your employees talk to you, they are asking you to effect change. If you ignore what they have to say and allow the status quo to remain intact, they will eventually either give up speaking with you altogether, or become disingenuous. At that point, you have an effective "communication breakdown" that may be incredibly difficult to correct.

Let me give you an actual example from an employee who now works for us: one day, this employee (then an assistant manager at another restaurant) told her general manager that she could not continue to work the hours he'd given her. The general manager nodded appreciatively every time she brought up the subject, but he did nothing. Apparently, he liked the schedule the way it was. Eventually, this assistant manager stopped bringing up the scheduling issues in their conversations. The general manager assumed that the problem was solved, and, in a way, it was: she had found another job which fit her new schedule, and she quit soon thereafter. Now this general manager was left with a really serious scheduling problem, mostly of his own making. He had listened, but he hadn't listened with the intention of making a change.

The same example applies to a dozen other scenarios: customers request that a certain item be carried, employees ask for extra help or tools, community groups ask for help with their events, and so forth. Whenever you take the time to listen, you can make the time to take action—not giving in every time, but proving that you can do something to make the situation better for both parties. Otherwise, when no change is initiated or no action is taken, you will "hear" a deafening silence and witness employee and customer defections that generally could have been avoided.

I firmly believe that listening is one of the most important skills we can learn, and I wish that we taught our young people listening as a discipline in high-school or college. With more diverse workforces and shorter attention spans, listening to change is more important than ever.

No task is ever so serious that we cannot have fun in the process. In the hospitality business, having fun is an important part of entertaining our customers; that makes it an integral part of the W.O.W. experience at Old San Francisco as well as at other successful dining places.

T.G.I. Friday's was one of the first restaurants to make having fun part of the corporate culture. Early on, executives made one very small decision: they allowed employees to wear whatever they wanted to on their heads. The uniform was still the uniform, from the neck down. But above the collar, employees could show all the individuality they desired.

Of course, the so-called "hat rule" was an extremely modest change in policy, but it became extremely important to T.G.I. Friday's culture. Why? The individual headgear created spontaneity. Employees not only had fun creating their own hats, but every day there was something new and crazier to look forward to. If every day at other restaurants was considered a grind, every day at T.G.I. Friday's was, in a way, like Halloween.

Southwest Airlines has taken the concept of fun much further. Their flight attendants know that they are not expected to be humorless meal distributors and FAA policy enforcers, but entertainers. I travel on Southwest Airlines several times a week, and I've hear countless jokes to make the flight that much more bearable. One of my favorites came about an hour into a flight, as the head flight attendant announced over the P.A. system: "There is a very special person on our flight today. He is

celebrating his 92nd birthday, and he's never been on an airplane before."
Of course, all of the passengers, including myself, applauded. But the joke
was on us. A few seconds later, as the plane began its descent, she said
"Thank you for the applause. When we land, I think that it would be nice if
each of you stopped to personally congratulate the captain on your way out
of the plane."

At Old San Francisco, we use fun to change similarly tedious
situations. For example, we usually cannot seat parties without reservations
immediately, so we end up with a lot of customers waiting for their table at
the bar, sometimes for over an hour. As anyone knows, waiting for a table
can be extremely boring. What's worse, people with reservations or parties
of a smaller size are being seated ahead of you, so you're watching
everyone else like a hawk to protect your place in line.

Our hosts break the ice by asking each waiting party to make the most
noise they can when their name is called; then everyone else who's waiting
for a table gets to judge whether or not they've shown enough enthusiasm to
be deserving of a table. Not only does this heighten the anticipation and
create constant entertainment while the minutes are ticking away, but the
game instills a sense of camaraderie in what can be a pretty hostile,
competitive situation. Fun is a terrific way to turn high-tense into high-
touch.

While fun is important, faith—both in yourself and in your people—is also essential to succeed in the long term. Faith fuels our consistent effort when times are at their most difficult.

Unfortunately, faith is not as simple as we would like to believe. It's certainly not easy, and it's never a matter of positive thinking alone. (If all we had to do was tell ourselves "I can!" to move forward, we'd all be hugely successful.) The difficult part is telling ourselves that, even if we cannot do it right now, we will be able to in the future—*if* we work hard enough, *if* we have patience, and *if* we never lose our faith in our ability to change into something better than we are today.

Anne Van Ness Farrell is one of the most successful women in America. She has been a super mother, wife, teacher, philanthropist, and businesswomen. Today, she serves as president of The Seattle Foundation. I once heard someone ask her how she'd been able to succeed in all of these very different disciplines. "You can have it all," she said, "but you can't have it all at the same time." In other words, even if you can't achieve something in the immediate, you should never lose your faith that you can accomplish it somewhere down the road.

Since none of us accomplishes anything alone, we must display the same faith in our people. We should never antagonize those responsible for building our success. If we lose our faith in certain people, they shouldn't be working with us; otherwise, they are automatically deserving of our trust. Of course, investing faith means committing the occasional mistake—honest or no—but that's minuscule compared to what's sacrificed when you say, in essence, "I don't trust anyone to do their job."

Tom Monaghan, the founder of Domino's Pizza, is probably the world's staunchest believer in the power of faith. An intensely religious man, Monaghan was raised an orphan by nuns whose faith in the young outcast transformed his life. Monaghan completely rejects the notion that some people are not deserving of faith, going so far as to credit his success to trusting employees and franchisees.

But exercising faith and getting results are, of course, two different issues. And Monaghan freely admits that faith accomplishes little without incentives. For example, he once offered a manager $50,000 to shed 80 pounds and run a marathon. While other managers scoffed at the idea that this person would completely change his lifestyle for any amount of money, Monaghan knew better. He knew that, by exercising a great deal of faith and a relatively small incentive, he could make this manager change his life.

We only give up when we lose hope. And I don't think we ever lose hope as long as we have faith that our efforts—individually and collectively—will be rewarded.

Understand Your Fears

If you can force your heart and nerve and sinew

To serve your turn long after they are gone,

And so hold on when there is nothing in you

Except the will which says to them: "Hold On!"

Rudyard Kipling

Gerry Spence is the best criminal lawyer in the country. He has never lost a case, including one where the accused shot a man at point blank range in front of five witnesses. He is the attorney who won a "not guilty" verdict for former Philippine First Lady Imelda Marcos after calling no witnesses in her defense, and despite the fact that the prosecutor—Rudy Giuliani (now mayor of New York)—had guaranteed a conviction.

Spence does whatever it takes to win. He has to. When he takes on a case, there are only two possible outcomes: guilty or not guilty. When he approaches the jury to make his final argument before a verdict is rendered, he is tired from months of hard work and little sleep, haunted by the thought of the person sitting next to him going to prison, and, as he freely admits, scared as hell.

So, as he clears his throat to deliver the argument which will either win his client's acquittal or secure a conviction, Spence always pauses for a few minutes to remind himself of how fearful he is. He thinks about everything that should cause total paralysis—any possible flaws in his delivery, a biased member of the jury, a brilliant presentation by the prosecution. And when he has finished confronting his fears, he moves on. And wins.

We face similar fears in the hospitality business; our jury is not 12 citizens but an endless stream of customers who judge us on our ability to achieve perfection. There are so many variables which can fail, making our customers angry, disappointing them, and even, in the food business, injuring them. But we cannot allow these fears to get the best of us; we must teach our people how, like Spence, to overcome their fears and face their audience in total confidence.

At Old San Francisco, each of our restaurants does a huge banquet and catering business. Everyone—from our managers to our employees—knows that these events are make or break for our company: either we will "W.O.W." the companies which entrust us with their special event, or we will disappoint them. To compound the potential problems, we are often forced to hire temporary employees to handle the extra business at certain times.

How have we taught them to deal with this pressure? Mostly, we have empowered them to do whatever it takes to make our customers' experiences a success. If a misstep happens, our servers are trained to rally around the mistake and turn it into a positive. If we can help out at the corporate level, we will also do whatever it takes. As an example, all of our employees are required to work on holidays, including myself. So when our servers venture out into the dining room to create a memorable experience for our guests, they know that the CEO is (literally) right behind them.

Perhaps the most agonizing dilemma of any leader is knowing when to step aside. In the hospitality business, where success is a function of so many people working together, "control freaks" rarely succeed. I have seen more than a few promising young businesses fail because their leaders, upon achieving some initial success, refused to let anyone else take over the reins. They became control freaks, not realizing that their future challenges would require completely different skills than those which made them successful.

George Naddaff is a terrific example of the opposite approach. Naddaff is the man who founded Boston Chicken. Boston Chicken, of course, has become one of the industry's fastest-growing companies, largely because Naddaff knew when to step aside. In 1992, he sold most of his interest in the "home-meal replacement" chain to a group of investors capable of injecting the necessary management and financing needed to make the company a national chain. Naddaff not only has no regrets for stepping aside when he did, he's already moved on to two more ventures: Silver Diner, and Tony Maroni's. Silver Diner has since become a successful public company, and Tony Maroni's may not be far behind.

Another terrific leader who knows when to step aside is Phil Romano, creator of numerous chains including Fuddrucker's, Macaroni Grill and Eatzi's. Romano is a creative genius whose penchant for anticipating trends and generating excitement is nothing short of legendary. But Romano has sold nearly every concept he's every started to a larger company capable of managing the growth for which he has laid the foundation.

While both Naddaff and Romano have stepped away from the helms of their respective concepts, neither has walked away from their creations entirely. Both serve as consultants and directors of the companies which currently own their concepts. And both remain psychologically attached to what they've created, knowing that stepping aside at the right time was an integral part of their ongoing success.

Change Before You're Forced To

The best time to make any change is before you're forced to by financial or operational issues. By anticipating major changes down the road, you allow yourself far more flexibility with which to meet future challenges. At Old San Francisco, we're determined to remain in control of our future by staying at least one step ahead of our customers, and two steps ahead of our competitors.

Last year, for example, we added emu and ostrich meats to most of our menus, even though we know that they will account for a minuscule percentage of sales. We also remodeled a couple of rooms that probably didn't need it, and we upgraded several of the steaks on our menu even though no customers complained—the quality was already superb. Conventional wisdom tells us to wait for a problem ("if it ain't broke, don't fix it!"), but by that time, we know it will be too late to be ahead of the game.

Are You Ready For Change? A Test

Preparing for the 21st century means being watchful, open and willing to changes, *especially* those which prove to be unexpected or uncomfortable. As much as I would like to believe otherwise, we are not all capable of leading change; many of us have too many emotional and financial investments in the status quo.

Are you prepared to lead change? Here is a simple test:

On a piece of paper, draw two columns. One column represents your investments—financial, emotional, and spiritual. The other column represents what you are willing to risk—in other words, what you are willing to lose. This column should include material things such as fancy cars, a monetary nest egg, and expensive dinners out, but also the less obvious assets such as certain relationships (which you may no longer have the time for), a sense of financial security, and extraneous parts of your identity (is it important for you to see yourself as a physician rather than a restaurateur? is a common example). You will probably find that these second considerations are far more important ones.

If what you are willing to risk is roughly equal to what you own, you are ready for change. If you are not willing to risk very much of what you have, you're not. Finally, if you are very eager to risk everything, you may be in serious danger of jumping onto any new opportunity, simply because you have nothing to lose.

Remember that change ultimately sheds much of your past identity, but also that it brings you much closer to your values—what some people call the "real you". Therefore, real change is impossible to force if your personal balance sheet is not already in check. You must be ready for change.

When Ray Kroc founded McDonald's, he was a 57-year-old milkshake salesman. When Ruth Fertel founded 65-unit Ruth's Chris Steakhouse, she was a thirty-something single mother with a little experience and an incredible will.

It is impossible to say what makes some of us successful, what makes caterpillars suddenly burst out into the open as butterflies. What is clear, however, is that we are all capable of changing—no matter how old, no matter how penniless, no matter how preoccupied with families or other commitments. Still, so many of us hold onto excuses; we convince ourselves that there is no hope, or that our own circumstances are somehow insurmountable. I think that Fertel, Kroc and countless other success stories disprove that notion.

In fact, hardship is usually one of the most telling precursors to success. Recently, I met with the founder and owner of an exploding chain of franchised pizza restaurants, whose experience mirrors my own in the franchise industry. Speaking of franchisees, he warned "don't go for the people with money. Choose people that are hungry, and you'll be successful."

How different that is from the conventional wisdom that we should find partners with money first, and worry about motivation later.

What causes the caterpillar to metamorphosize is not a comfortable resting place, but a hunger to renew itself, to change into something capable of far more. The hospitality industry is already undergoing a profound metamorphosis. We can either ignore it, or we can transform ourselves to meet the new challenges and opportunities. None of us faces obstacles so great that we cannot W.O.W. ourselves into the 21st century, which is precisely what we need to do, starting today.

The caterpillar doesn't know that he'll come out as a butterfly.

All he knows is that he's alone, it's dark, and it's a little scary.

Mort Meyerson, Perot Systems

Tomorrow is already here. The wheels of change are already spinning. By ignoring them or misinterpreting their direction, we risk failure. The answer? Knowledge. Then action.

Knowledge doesn't need to be high-tech—you don't need a relational database to know who your customers are. As Rich Melman says, "The best market research is getting out and talking to people."

But knowing your customers, as well as your employees, vendors and communities, does require an investment of high-touch—an investment which is leveraged by consistent effort and renewed by W.O.W. practices.

Rather than wrap things up at the end, like most books, I've made a few high-touch suggestions to help you create a new beginning—to achieve your own version of Mort Meyerson's metamorphosis. Here goes:

- Find out a personal concern of one of your employees.

- Find out a personal concern of one of your customers.

- Call a customer or client to just say "thank you" for their business.

- Note an anniversary—that of an employee, a vendor, or customer.

- Discover one way in which your employees are "beating the system."

- Start discussing a co-op advertising plan with a supplier who currently

  offers none.

- Figure out a promotion that your competitors would never do, and do it.

- Ask your employees to design an incentive program for themselves.

- Send someone who fuels your success a bouquet of flowers.

Following are some photos of high-touch activities we've recently created at Old San Francisco. Call me tomorrow, and I'll be able to send you more.

Barry Cohen

*...Speaking at the party we hosted for the
no longer stranded Olympic volunteers. . .*

*...Helping drop off boxed lunches at the "drive-thru" we created for cab drivers
in San Antonio to say "thank you". . .*

...We love anniversaries, whether for our restaurants, long-time employees, or even long-time customers. . .

. . .Speaking at an event we created for
The Restaurant & Purveyor of the Year awards.. . .

. . .Celebrating with customers in our Nob Hill Crystal Room in San Antonio. . .

. . .The new Mud King and Queen Susan Neiman with the mayor of San Antonio. . .

*. . .And the rewards of it all! A tiny sampling of the
many letters of thanks we receive every day at Old San Francisco.
These letters are the cornerstone of our business. . .*

A Van-Gogh-esque portrait we had done of one of our steakhouses. . .

. . .Finally, back in the office. I'm probably arranging another promotion. . .

*. . .Celebrating the launch of our lunch menu in Dallas
with motivational guru Zig Ziglar. . .*

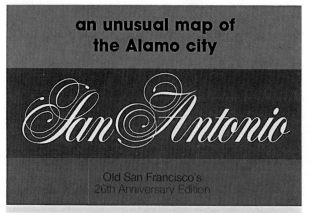

an unusual map of
the Alamo city

San Antonio

Old San Francisco's
26th Anniversary Edition

. . .Our custom guide to San Antonio--not surprisingly, Old San Francisco Steakhouse stands out prominently above the rest. The same can be said of our food and service . .

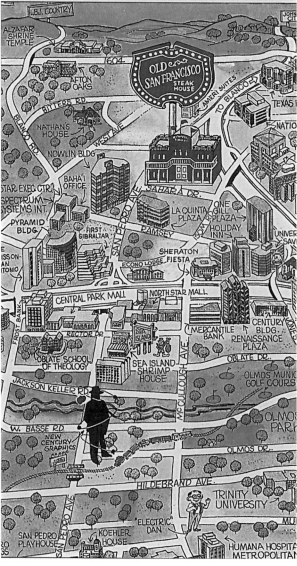

≈♡≈ DINE OUT TEXAS ≈♡≈

"*If they love us when they leave us, they'll be back. To make customers LOVE you, everything has to be perfect.* That's why we welcome the American Express® Card."

≈♡≈

Barry Cohen/Chief Executive Officer
Cardmember since 1979

Old San Francisco Steak & Seafood House
Four locations in Texas
For the location nearest you, call (210) 341-3189
American Express® Cardmembers
welcomed since 1968

Don't Leave Home Without It.

≈♡≈

© 1995 American Express Travel Related Services Company, Inc.

. . .A co-op ad we did with American Express, stating one of my favorite principles. Your suppliers can be some of your best marketing partners—this particular ad ran a full page in the Wall Street Journal!. . .

CERTIFICATE
OF MERIT

Presented to

_____

For your Spirit, Desire, Determination,
and Commitment as a Team Player
who is focused on Cost Containment
and Reduction

_____
Date

_____   _____
Old San Francisco Steak House   AmeriClean Systems Inc.

...Turning dishwashers into cost-managers: our award certificate, sponsored by AmeriClean Systems. .

Barry M. Cohen leads the foodservice industry in cutting-edge marketing strategies and management techniques.

Currently Chief Executive Officer of Old San Francisco Steak House Corporation, Cohen joined its management team in 1989 as General Manager of the San Antonio restaurant. In 1993 he was appointed C.E.O. of the parent corporation for the Old San Francisco Steak Houses in Austin, Dallas, Houston and San Antonio.

In addition to his management duties, Cohen appears occasionally as Guest Chef on television programs such as Robin Leech's TV Food Network and KSAT-12's morning news, leading to ABC's "Good Morning America". His descriptive verbal skills and wit also enable him to "prepare" breakfast for radio listeners on such programs as KSMG Radio's popular morning show.

Cohen has served in a wide range of national and local civic and community organizations. His involvement in the San Antonio region alone included board positions with the American Heart Association, the Greater San Antonio Chamber of Commerce, the San Antonio Restaurant Association and Sales and Marketing Executives of San Antonio. He is past Vice President and Chairman for "Taste of San Antonio", an annual event where area restaurants showcase their finest dishes.

In 1996, Cohen was presented with the Sales and Marketing Executives of San Antonio 's coveted Pinnacle Award. He was also named 1996 "Shoe Leather Marketer of the Year" by *Restaurant Marketing*, an influential international newsletter. His innovative promotions have been the subject of articles in numerous publications, including *ADWEEK* and the *San Antonio Express-News*. Mr. Cohen has published articles on W.O.W. marketing *in Nation's Restaurant News* and *The Cornell Quarterly*, among other publications. He is a co-author of "50 Proven Ways To Build Restaurant Sales & Profit".

As an innovative Epicurean, Cohen has received numerous awards for his original recipes, including national awards from the national Egg Council, Dole Pineapple Company and the National Strawberry Council. He placed in The Great Chefs of Texas competition sponsored by the Texas Department of Agriculture.

ABOUT OLD SAN FRANCISCO

*Old San Francisco was founded in 1968, in San Antonio, to greet guests
of that year's World's Fair. Today, we operate high-volume restaurants in
Dallas, Houston, Austin, San Antonio and Las Vegas.*

STEAKS & SEAFOOD

Did you borrow this book? Do you want a copy of your own? Do you need extra copies for your staff and management? Would you like information on bringing W.O.W. 2000 to your next meeting or convention?

BOOK ORDER

Yes! I want to invest in my future success and have a personal copy of *"W.O.W. 2000"*.

1-19 copies: $15.00 each plus postage & handling*

20+ copies: call for discount information

No. Copies _____

Total Amount
of Order $_____

Postage & Handling
MUST BE ADDED TO ALL ORDERS
Figure postage & handling at the greater of $5.00* or 6% of the total book order.

Method of Payment: ☐ Check ☐ Money Order ☐ VISA
☐ MC ☐ Amex

Account No. _____

Expires _____ **Signature** _____

*Canadian funds: $20.00 + postage & handling (greater of $6.00 or 8% of book order)
Allow 30 days for delivery on all orders

What topics would you like to see addressed in future books?

_____

return to: Savannah Corp./Old San Francisco
2601 Hibernia St. • Suite B
Dallas, TX 75204
TEL: 888-OSFSHCO
FAX 214-754-8067

Barry M. Cohen has inspired audiences from hospitality executives to telephone engineers with his "W.O.W. 2000" message. If you would like speaking information, please tell us the following:

Name of Organization/Company: _____

How many People Will Be Attending? _____

Probable Date and Location: _____

Please Describe Your Primary Area of Interest (e.g. marketing): _____

SEND BOOKS AND INFORMATION TO:

Name _____

Company _____

Address _____

City _____ State _____ Zip _____

Phone _____ Fax _____

e-mail _____